Souvenirs
of a
SuperAger

Stories from My Life

ALAIN F. CORCOS

Souvenirs of a SuperAger: Stories from My Life

Copyright © 2023 Alain F. Corcos. All rights reserved. No part of this book may be reproduced or retransmitted in any form or by any means without the written permission of the publisher.

Published by Wheatmark®
2030 East Speedway Boulevard, Suite 106
Tucson, Arizona 85719 USA
www.wheatmark.com

ISBN: 979-8-88747-082-5 (paperback)
ISBN: 979-8-88747-083-2 (ebook)
LCCN: 2023907884

Bulk ordering discounts are available through Wheatmark, Inc. For more information, email orders@wheatmark.com or call 1-888-934-0888.

To my former students and my friends,
in particular Mike and Katie,
who pushed me to write these stories.

Introduction

I am living a long life and I have a lot of stories to tell. Many of my friends who have heard my stories, have encouraged me to write them down. Some of these stories are unique and could only have happened to me because I was born and raised in France, escaped from Nazi France three months before D-Day with my brother Gilles, joined the French Air Force, and passed all my adulthood in the United States.

When I go back to France on vacation, I feel like a fish out of water. After so many years of living in the States, I've found that I have forgotten the customs of my original country—or perhaps those customs have changed. Speaking French like a Frenchman, I have found myself in strange situations. For example, my American wife and I were once at the Orly airport, south of Paris. We decided to have some sandwiches before taking off for America. There was an American couple ordering ahead of us at the café who did not speak French. After they left, the server, having no notion that I was American, expressed his unflattering opinion about this couple in particular and Americans in general. I did not try to change his opinion. Another time I was helping my wife buy some perfume in Paris and the owner of the shop told me in English that I was speaking French very well for an American.

Though my brother Gilles and I were born in Paris, we were raised on the French Rivera, next to Menton, which is a border town between France and Italy. Our home was a spacious villa, called *Clair Matin* (Clear Morning), and located in the center of a flower farm extending over fifteen acres in the terraced hills overlooking Menton.

At the time of our move from Paris to the region of Roquebrune-Cap-Martin, the population was small—about 6,000 people—with a colorful history. In pre-Roman times the area was settled by the Ligurians, also known as the people who now occupy Italy. Traces of their language can still be found in the local dialect. The commune (originally known as Roccabruna) was founded in 971 by Conrad I, Count of Ventimiglia, in order to protect his western border. In1355, Roccabruna fell under the control of the Grimaldi family of Monaco for five centuries during which time the medieval castle was strengthened. Centuries later in 1793, Roquebrune became French.

A revolution of the Italian Risorgimento broke out in 1848, resulting in Roccabruna and Menton becoming free cities under the protection of the Savoy Prince. However, their independence lasted only two years and they were then put under the Savoyan administration (nominally still under the Prince of Monaco).They remained in a state of political limbo from 1849 until they finally ceded to France by a plebiscite in 1861.

Today, Roquebrune-Cap-Martin has several villages and towns: St.Roman, which is practically a suburb of Monaco (but not part of Monaco proper, as it does not lie within Monaco's borders), as well as the residential areas of Cabbe, Bon Voyage, and Serret. Roquebrune delights with its perched village and chateau, the posh Cap Martin peninsula, and the modern seaside of Carnoles, which features a long pebble beach bordering Menton.[1]

Growing up in Southern France, Gilles and I acted like the children around us to the dismay of our mother, who was born and raised in Paris.We even talked like them—we still have the French Southern accent, which God knows is much different from the sophisticated "Parisian" accent. We used local expressions known only to those who lived in "La Provence."Our Mother did not blame this on the fact that we were raised in the region, but instead on the fact that we often repeated word for word in the accent of Provence, the everlasting films of Marcel Pagnol, including *Marius*, *Fanny*, and *César*.These witty films told the story of three generations of a family from Marseille using their vernacular. Gilles and I adopted the customs of the French Riviera and have told its colorful stories our whole lives.

If Gilles and I passed our youth in France, we have passed the rest of our lives in the United States. We are both retired after years of teaching and researching as university professors—Gilles in engineering and I in Botany.

---

1 In the famous1948 film *The Red Shoes,* the lovers are kissing each other in a fiacre. They do not know where they are and do not care. But I know. They are going around Cap Martin.

Some of my stories happened in France, while others took place in the United States. These stories are still clear in my mind. Some are very short; some are longer.

The most important story in my life was my escape from Nazi France in March 1944. For many years I told the story of my escape to my friends and colleagues. Many times they suggested that I write down the story; however, I never had the time until I was nearly retired. I wrote a first draft of about 25 pages and gave it to some of my best students to read. They asked me the strangest questions: Why did you leave? Did your mother cry when you left? Only a female student could ask such a question. I was bewildered by these questions and could not understand why they did not know the horrific conditions of occupied Europe during World War II.

Even my best students did not understand why my brother and I left occupied Europe. This was because they had very little, if any, knowledge of World War II. They had no sense of war. I suppose this is good in one sense and bad in another. It quickly became obvious that I had to include a lot of history in my book and describe our lives in France from 1940 to 1944. This was easy because I lived it and remembered it well. So, in my book, *The Little Yellow Train*, I describe in detail why the Vichy government, the French government of the time, was in some ways more Nazi and anti-Semitic than the German government. Since I wrote *The Little Yellow Train*, historians not only confirmed this, but some have also gone beyond even what I recounted.

Back to the question of why my mother didn't cry when her sons left her for an uncertain future. Well, she did what any mother would have done at the time: help her children take the road to freedom so that they would not die in labor camps under the Allied forces' bombs. My parents did not have time to cry—they had shed all their tears long before our trip. So, with the help of the underground, they sent my brother and I on our way to Spain and an uncertain future.

I have to confess that over the three months I wrote that book, I had a personal crisis. I could not write a specific chapter, which I entitled "Vichy, The Jews and Us." The reason was simple—I was re-living a part of my life I wanted to forget. According to the Nazis, anyone who had Jewish ancestry, was a Jew and was destined to be exterminated. My family has Jewish ancestry, but had not practiced the Jewish faith for several generations—I do not know anything about the rites of Judaism.

In order to survive we never played the game that the Vichy government wanted us to play—*tell us you are a Jew and we will kill you.* We left our home. We forged papers. Our parents hid in various villages under assumed names until the liberation. While our immediate family survived the Holocaust intact, I unfortunately lost two uncles, two aunts, and two cousins. You can read more about this part of my history in *The Little Yellow Train.*

1

Growing Up in France

I Could Have Died

My first adventure was being born. Some might think that was the easy part, but I had a brain hemorrhage when I was born. The doctor who delivered me said I was not going to live, but no one believed him. My mother's sister took care of me and eventually my hemorrhage stopped and I have lived to become a superager. Superager is a new word in the English language, which describes people over 85 years of age. Some of them (including me) have a very good memory and remember much of what happened in their lives very well. Recently, a study has shown that superagers have larger neurons in the section of the brain that has to do with memory.

For example, I very clearly remember a plane crash in Paris when I was only five years old. I also remember riding in a Model-T Ford truck at seven years old in 1932. That same year I remember witnessing an earthquake that hit my hometown of Menton—a very rare occurrence.

When I decided to write to write a book of the stories that my listeners found most interesting, I did not include what happened to me and my family during World War II. That can be read in my book, *The Little Yellow Train, Survival and Escape from Nazi France (June 1940 – March 1944)*. Instead, these are stories about growing up in the 1930s and 40s, attending university in the 1950s, and working and teaching in the 1960s and through the 1980s.

I tried to put the stories in some kind of order, but it is difficult because I have been a lot of places. To help with a timeline, I'll give you a brief history of where I was before settling in East Lansing, Michigan. I was born in Paris (France, not Ohio) and was raised on the French Riviera. I escaped from Vichy France and enlisted in the French Air Force in Casablanca, Morocco as a teenager. I first came to the United States to be trained as a pilot. It turned out that my depth perception was so bad that I was never able to even start the program. Instead I became a clerk and an interpreter.

When the war was over, I went back to France and took over the family flower farm where I discovered that raising carnations requires far too much work, so I decided to go back to the States to learn more efficient ways to cultivate plants. I never returned to France to live after that. I started my college life at San Luis Obispo, California, where I attended a very practical college called Cal Poly. I switched from being a special student to a regular one. Then I moved from San Luis Obispo to East Lansing. I got my B.S. and M.S. in Botany and Plant Pathology, and my Ph.D. in plant breeding from Michigan State University. My first professional job was peach breeding at Red Bluff, California. My second was as a lab instructor at the new campus of the University of California at Santa Barbara, which was a temporary position. I was offered a regular position as instructor at the College of Education in the little town of Monmouth, Oregon. I stayed there only one year because I was offered a research associate position at the University of Michigan in the summer of 1964 and at the Fox Chase Institute for Cancer Research in Philadelphia. In that building, all the offices had water, gas, electricity, and a member of the Academy of Sciences. I finally got a permanent position when I returned to MSU as a faculty member teaching the nature and philosophy of science and doing research in plant biology, which I did for 26 years. I retired as a professor emeritus in plant biology.

Plane Crash in Paris

As I previously mentioned, my brother Gilles and I were born in Paris, with the first years of our life spent at Neuilly, a suburb of Paris. I do not remember much about this time except a Christmas party and our learning to ride bicycles, but there is something we will never forget. We were in the garden at the back of our house when we saw a small plane crashing in the streets. I believe it happened in 1930 when there were very few planes in the sky. The chances of seeing a plane crash were very small, but we definitely did. The plane twisted around as it fell. Although we were very young—four- and five-years-old, respectively—we never forgot that crash. Ironically, this did not prevent us from joining the French Air Force in March 1944.

Another Plane Crash

Years later, once our family was established on the French Riviera, Father heard that his brother Fernand was coming to see us. He was taking a plane from Paris to Nice. Father went to pick him up from the airport, but upon arrival, he learned that the plane had crashed. Completely upset, he read the names of the passengers who had perished and could not find

Fernand's name. He was told that there was another plane coming in an hour, so Father waited for its arrival. One of the first passengers to leave the plane was Fernand, who told his brother that "he never takes a plane that is going to crash."

Search for Paradise

In 1932, Father decided that he was retiring from running his own business and my parents began their search for a home on the French Riviera. They first looked near St. Tropez, which was practically uninhabited at that time. No one could predict that billionaires would one day have beautiful homes in that region. Mother thought that we would be too isolated there, so my parents moved their search nearer to the Italian border.

One morning they found their dream home. As mother approached the gate of the property she called to my father and said, "Maurice, we got it."[2] She was right. It was a beautiful place. Not only was the house very nice, but the garden had all kinds of fruits, including fig trees to cherry trees. To their surprise, my parents found out that *"Clair Matin,"* the name of the villa, was a flower farm, with the main product being carnations. My parents had no idea how to grow carnations, but were lucky enough to find an Italian family that knew the business and moved into the second house on our property. Coincidentally the name of that family was Profumo (Perfume), a proper name for a family that grows flowers.

---

2   Falling in love with houses is common. Personally it happened to me when I was in Oregon and in Michigan when I bought a cottage on the shore of Wiggins Lake in Gladwin County.

The Republic is in Danger

When I heard about the attack on the United States Capitol on January 6, 2021, I immediately thought of two attacks on the French Republic by extremist right wingers. One in 1934, and the other during the Algerian war. To me, such attacks are nothing new. We have to be ready to defend our democratic countries at all times!

From 1934 to 1939, France teetered on the brink of civil war. Unfortunately, it seems that France is always on the verge of some political upheaval. On the one hand, the right wing was fearful that the communists would seize power. On the other hand, the left wing was afraid that the extreme right would topple the republic. On the evening of February 6, 1934, I overheard the strangest telephone conversation between Father who was in Paris and Mother who was at home with me. It went like this:

Father: Well. It was very serious.
Mother: Oh. It was.
Father: Did you hear about it?
Mother: Of course. It was terrible.
Father: There were a lot of casualties.
Mother: No! There were none.
Father: Of course, there were a lot on the bridge.
Mother: What are you talking about, the bridge?
Father: The Concorde Bridge over the Seine.

It finally dawned on them that they were talking about two

different things. Mother was talking about a very violent, windy storm that toppled many trees on our hills, while Father was talking about the unsuccessful march of some 40,000 right wing demonstrators on the Assembly. The demonstrators were stopped by police on the Concorde Bridge over the Seine, which was within a block of the parliament building. It had been a bloody battle for a few hours, but the republic had been saved.

Years later, the French Republic was again in danger. It was during the Algerian war, which was fought between France and the Algerian National Liberation. The war lasted from 1954 to 1962, and led to Algeria winning its independence from France. But not everyone in Algeria accepted the French withdrawal. This included the *Pieds-Noirs* (people of French and other European-decent born in Algeria during the French rule) and members of the French Army. In fact, they tried to overthrow the French government, but were unsuccessful because the French Air Force, who was needed to bring paratroopers to Paris, refused to participate in the overthrow.

Politics in Southern France

In 1936, changes occurred in the leadership of our local government. Earlier that year Father had been asked to add his name to a list of people who, dissatisfied with the way the commune (township) was administered, thought they could do a better job. They thought that Father, having been a successful businessman, would be an asset in managing the business of the community. After some reflection, he decided to accept the challenge.

In France people are not elected on an individual basis, but as members of a political group. To his astonishment, Father and his newly found friends had been elected by a landslide and he found himself as the vice-mayor of the commune. For the first time in his life he was an official in the community in which he lived. Gilles and I were very proud of him, though we did not know exactly what his job consisted of. A few months later, we were told that among his official duties he had the authority to perform marriages. To us children, this was really impressive.

The day after the election, our parents were sitting on the front terrace of our house when they heard a three-man band playing drums, saxophone, and trumpet. The music was not too bad—some of the tunes were even recognizable. Soon the band appeared on the terrace and continued to play for a few minutes. Shortly, Father realized that it was a local tradition for new members of the council to be serenaded, and Mother realized that she had better get some glasses and wine to celebrate her husband's election. The trumpeter, Mr. Vial, was a character who lived at the top of our hill and was well-known for spending every franc he made on wine. But he really knew how to play the trumpet—one of his official jobs was to play the trumpet on the Fourteenth of July, which is the day the French people celebrate their liberation from the tyranny of the King. It was on that day in 1789, that they stormed the Bastille, where the King's enemies were jailed for years without trial.

The mayor of the commune did not want Mr. Vial to be drunk for the celebration, so every year on the eve of Bastille Day, he had him put in jail. The next day, a sober Mr. Vial would play the trumpet and patriotic speeches would be made in the Place des Freres square in the old Roquebrune-Cap-Martin village.

Classical Music

Father loved to listen to recordings of classical music in his big study. He played his music on one of the most modern phonographs of the time.For years he did not have a radio because he found it unnecessary. However, his brother Fernand thought otherwise. After all, the world was in turmoil and my father should be informed. So one day in 1937, Uncle Fernand, who was visiting at *Clair Matin* for a few days, asked me for a good-looking envelope and the best writing paper in the house. Then in his superb hand writing he wrote the following:

> *My Dear Brother,*
>
> *Throw your d . . . phonograph through the window and buy yourself the most expensive radio you can find.*
>
> *Love,*
>
> *Fernand*

Then he gave me the letter and told me to give it to Father as soon as he left town—which I did. Father did not throw his phonograph through the window, but he did buy a radio and discovered that for years he had been missing the outstanding classical music programs played from Radio Monte Carlo.

Fernand Buys a Piece of *Clair Matin*

My Uncle Fernand enjoyed spending time with us on the French Riviera. So much so that he decided to buy a piece of *Clair Matin*, but was not going to tell us its location. He wanted to buy two square meters so he could move his chair to follow the sun all day. Of course there was never any sale and my uncle was welcome to put his chair anywhere he wanted.

Six White Carnations

Although the climate is mild year round on the French Riviera, very few carnations bloom in January. This fact did not prevent a man in charge of a wedding in Monaco from calling us. The future bride he was working for wanted at least six white carnations for her wedding. He told us that the price was of no concern. Even before Grace Kelly became the princess of Monaco, it was known to be the home of the richest men and women. My father agreed and went to see if he could find some white carnations for the bride. This was not an easy task because we had more than 100,000 carnations on our farm. After two hours of searching, Father had finally found them and called the man in charge of the wedding. Someone came and picked up the very special flowers, making the future bride very happy.

The Fig

My parents had a painter friend who lived in the old village of Roquebrune and loved to tell stories. I heard a few of his stories, including this one. In a village in North Africa there was a custom to elect someone as the laziest man in town. A man and his little boy were talking when the man asked the little boy what he wanted to be when he grew up. The little boy answered that he wanted to be the laziest man in town. His father was very disappointed and told him so, but the little boy insisted.

Finally the father told his son that they had to visit the current laziest man in town to see whether the little boy had the talent to be one. So they went and the little boy was told to lie down next to the lazy man under a fig tree that dropped a fig or two from time to time. One fell on the cheek of the lazy man and he picked it up to eat it. But when a fig fell onto the little boy, he did not reach for the fig, and instead left it on his cheek. Finally, he told his father to put the fig in his mouth for him. The laziest man excitedly got up and worshipped the boy, calling him "Master….."

Local Food

The French Riviera, or *La Côte d'Azur*, is known for its charm, climate, gardens, and beaches, but it's also for famous for its local food dishes. Among them are the *panbagna* and the *pissaladière*.

In the local dialect, *pan* means "bread" and *bagna* means "bathed." This regional sandwich is not bathed in water, but in virgin olive oil. To make a *panbagna*, you cut a loaf of bread lengthwise into two parts. Then, you lay slices of juicy red tomatoes full of vitamins A and D, a few black anchovies, and a few slices of onion or garlic on the top of one of the half loaves. Then you pour enough olive oil on the top so that the oil soaks into the bread, but not enough soak through the crust. You then place the other half of the loaf on top of the of the first. This sandwich is eaten best with two hands, preferably sitting outside with your head slightly bent and your knees separated in order to prevent the dripping oil from staining your clothes.

From time to time, I prepare a *panbagna*, which I eat with a smile while remembering my youth on the French Riviera. I have known for a long time now that such a sandwich does marvels for your health. I instinctively knew what has only recently been confirmed—that olive oil lowers one's cholesterol and reduces the chances for heart attacks.

The other French dish, the *pissaladière*, became very popular in the United States starting in the 1950s, under the name "pizza." But let's face it—the original made on the French or Italian Riviera is far better than the U.S. imposter—not so much because of its contents, but because of its dough, which reminds any real connoisseur of the nature of French bread.

Hunting in Provence

Though the hills above my childhood home, *Clair Matin*, were rich with wild plants and crickets that chirped through the spring nights, they had no blackbirds, partridges, or rabbits to the despair of the local hunters. Yet from time to time, especially on Sunday afternoons, we could hear gunshots. Were the local hunters shooting their own caps, like the famous hunters of the illustrious town of Tarascon, north of Marseilles? No, they were mostly shooting at lizards and small snakes. I think they were also on the lookout for the legendary *tournepatte*. The *tournepatte* is a local bird whose right leg is shorter than its left leg due to the fact that it is always sitting on the side of the hill, facing south to enjoy the sun. Once you have located a *tournepatte*, it's very easy to get one. All you have to do is to imitate the sound of a gunshot and the terrified bird will turn around. Since it has one leg shorter than the other, it falls on its head and all that it is left to do is pick it up.

Bowling in Southern France

In 1938, a longtime friend of my parents, called Fernand Roccofort, bought the flower farm next door to us. He joined our *pétanque* team. In Southern France, the *pétanque*—similar to the Italian game of *bocce*—is the local pastime of the French who are known to play the game everywhere. In all the public squares and side streets of the provincial towns, games of *pétanque* can be found. Streetcars have even been known to stop so as to not interrupt games.

Father had converted part of one terrace into a *pétanque* court On a Sunday afternoon as Roccofort was playing *pétanque* with us, a man who was the local *rebouteux* (non-licensed chiropractor) was with us and asked him why he was limping. Roccofort told him that he had broken his ankle during a skiing trip and that he had it set by a famous surgeon in Paris, but ever since then he had a limp. The *rebouteux* told him to sit in a chair, and without asking permission, he pulled Roccofort's foot, twisting the ankle until he heard the sound of a bone snapping into place. Monsieur Roccofort yelled like a pig in a slaughterhouse, but to his stupefaction he discovered that his ankle did not hurt anymore. Within the hour he could walk like an ordinary human again. Welcome to the sophisticated unlicensed chiropractic art of the French Riviera.

Monsieur Tourdes

Italy declared war on France in June 1940, and in doing so, annexed Menton and its suburbs. We were told to leave and go somewhere else. Most of us in the area went to Antibes, an old Greek town west of Nice. My parents bought a rose farm where my brother and I would work and then attend high school in Antibes. The man who had sold the rose farm to my parents was a character. His name was Tourdes, and though he could not read or write, he was a very good business man and made a lot of money. I never forgot the way he would put his left index finger and thumb to his nose and while rubbing it and would say to my father, "If one of us dies, this would not be *cocagne*." This term is not French; but rather a provincial word, which means funny.

As I mentioned, Mr. Tourdes knew how to make money. When the liberation of France came in August 1944, my father sold the rose farm back to him. Tourdes made two lots out of the property and then sold them, making another bundle. I learned that education and smartness are two different things.

A Car that Did Not Want to Die

Before World War II, we had a Model A Ford that Father used to haul carnation baskets to the railway station of Menton. There our carnations would be sold in the early morning to flower merchants in Paris. The Model A was special because its back opened like the gate of the future station wagons. During the war, there was no gasoline for the Model A, and we had to transport everything by bicycle, including the flower baskets. They were put into a light homemade trailer that was hitched to the back of our bicycles. It was this velo-trailer that replaced the Model A Ford.

Father decided to hide the Model A under ten feet of carnation baskets. To be sure that no one would steal it, he took the wheels off and the battery out and stored them at a friend's home. The story of this car that we lovingly called "*La Rouge*" because of its outstanding red color, should be told. No other car I have known was ever built to last like this one.

When the liberation of France came in 1944, Father put the tires back on *La Rouge*, installed the battery, and called the local Ford garage to have the car towed and checked. The garage asked if he had started the engine. Father had not— who would believe that after four years the car would start on its own? He cranked the engine and it started right up. *La Rouge* took off and Father drove it to the Ford garage just to be told that it was perfectly fine. Father still did not drive the car much after the liberation, for there was still very little gasoline to be had.

In 1950 when my parents decided to immigrate to the United States (because Gilles and I were there), they decided to sell *La Rouge* to a young man in town. The young man had never owned a car and did not know to put oil in the crankcase from time to time.He soon ruined the engine, which was a rather inglorious death for such a marvelous car. Father should have kept it as an antique, a tribute to Quality One of the Ford Motor Company,

Wet Socks

When we were ten- and nine-years old, my brother Gilles and I passed the month of August with our parents in the mountains of Switzerland, where it was much cooler than on the French Riviera. Our mother could not stand the August heat—air conditioning did not exist back then. Gilles and I soon became mountain climbers.

Our parents and some of their friends decided to climb a famous peak called Arola. The first part of our adventure was to reach a hut, which was the halfway point of our climb. There we would pass the night and ready ourselves to reach the top of the mountain early in the morning before the ice melted. The problem with this was that there was nothing in the hut and had to bring everything we would need with us, including the wood needed to keep us warm during the night. At a dark 5 o'clock in the morning, our guide woke us up. The only light was from our flashlights.

We were offered some coffee before our trek, and then someone said he could not find one of his socks. We searched for his sock—finding it in the big coffee pot. This would not have been funny except that in French we have an expression to describe very bad coffee: "*jus de chaussette,*" or in English, "sock juice." That morning we really had drank *jus de chaussette*. This little mishap did not prevent us from reaching the top of the mountain. My brother was even recorded as the youngest climber of Arola.

Surgery, Anyone?

Climbing mountains like Arola can be dangerous as is demonstrated in this next story, which we heard from the restaurant owner at the village at the base of the mountain.

A group of ten people were at the top of the mountain when one of them slid and fell head first on to some small icy rocks. He was really in bad shape, but fortunately, another man in the group was a surgeon and took command of the situation. The wounded man was brought down the mountain very carefully, and once in the restaurant, the surgeon decided to do his best to treat the patient while waiting for an ambulance. The owner of the restaurant gave us details of the surgery, including the fact that they had to put the patient to sleep by giving him a lot of alcohol. There is no doubt that the surgeon had saved the life of his companion—you must remember that we did not have antibiotics to treat infections at that time.

Goggle Diving in Infancy

Gilles and I studied diligently at school, worked hard on the farm, but also had fun. During the spring of 1942, Father gave us a small sailing boat, about twelve feet long and three feet wide, with only one sail. He thought that it would be fun for his two boys to have a boat. But there was also a practical reason for his gift: he thought that we would use it to go fishing. With luck we should have been able to catch some seafood to put on the table for dinner. We did get fish, however, we didn't catch them with fishing rods, but rather by a new method called goggle diving. Goggle diving preceded scuba diving, which was invented and introduced by Captain Jacques Cousteau in 1943, a year after Gilles and I had taken up goggle diving on our own.

The idea of swimming, diving, and doing all kinds of things underwater was very challenging to us. So, how did we do it? We needed a watertight glass mask through which we could see and a snorkel tube through which we could breathe as we floated face down in the water, admiring sea landscapes and spotting fish. We also needed the means to kill a fish if we saw one. Since there was no equipment of this sort for purchase at the time, we had to make it ourselves or have it made—which is exactly what we did. The mask was cut out of a large innertube tire, with the front framed by an aluminum circle used for closing large glass jars.

Two rubber gas stove hoses were inserted into the sides of the mask so we could breathe. In order to prevent water from getting into our masks while diving, we inserted two ping pong balls into the hoses. The ping pong balls were secured by inserting two reed rods of just the right diameter into the ends of each rubber hose. This homemade mask permitted us to dive with ease.

The primitive snorkel was not too hard to make and was certainly not expensive. However, we had to turn to a professional for the next piece of equipment: the fishing gun, which could have also been called a slingshot. This weapon consisted of a broomstick with a hooked arrow fastened to one end. The arrow had to be made by a blacksmith and was the most expensive part of our equipment. The broomstick was propelled by a long narrow strip of rubber, cut out of an innertube. Both ends of the rubber strip were attached to the other end of the broomstick, and were only half as long as the broomstick. To propel our homemade slingshot, we put our wrist through the fold of the rubber strip, and then grip the front end of the broomstick as far as the rubber strip would permit us. When we saw prey, we would let go of the broomstick, which would slingshot forward.It did not move quickly nor go very far, but it worked! Fish did not hear or see the broomstick coming toward them underwater.

Though we had not heard of Frederic Dumas, Captain Cousteau's colleague, known as the best goggle diver of France, we were more or less using his technique to dive. We would start by bending from the waist and pointing our heads and torsos down. Then we would throw our legs up in the air with a powerful snap and down we would go. We were not as good as Dumas, who could go down 60 feet—our record was only about 30 feet, but we had lots of fun seeing underwater. A few times we were even able to add some seafood to the dinner table—a treat for the whole family.

Along with fishing, our boat also allowed us to inspect every nook and cranny along the Cap d'Antibes peninsula. One day we came inside a little beach belonging to the famous resort, Villa-Eden Roc, which was known for its swimming pool that used to glitter with Hollywood stars. Someone on the rocks nearby yelled to us that it was a private beach and we'd better leave. And private it was, because to our astonishment, we saw a woman and a man without a stitch on, swimming without shame around our boat. This was our first experience seeing nudists on a beach. We left slowly with the wind blowing in the sail.

Being a teenager is a difficult period of life, because it is the time of dawning sexual awareness. It is the time when boys consciously or unconsciously want to impress girls. Gilles and I were no exception. One day the chance to show off materialized. From Juan Les Pins beach we saw some girls sunbathing on the top of the limestone rocks that edged the beach and hung over the sea. We climbed to where the beauties were lying and then ran along past them and impulsively dove into the sea. As we were falling, it seemed to us that our descent through the air was taking quite a while. Later we found that we were right—we had dove from close to 50 feet. We were fortunate to be all right except for our faces and necks, which took a beating. We obviously succeeded beyond our imagination in impressing the girls, for they jumped to their feet and made it the cliff's edge in time to see us surface. I suppose that the young ladies were impressed not so much by our athletic abilities, but by our stupidity for not having realized how high those rocks were. In any case, we never jumped from them again.

The Art of Skiing

For a time my brother and I were high school borders at Briançon. One pleasure we partook in while we were there was skiing. Because of its location in the High Alps, Briançon and its surroundings were already a center for skiing in the 1940s. Living in such a place was great for us—we had been skiing since we were five- and six-years-old. A few miles from Briançon at Serres Chevalier, there was a ski lift, or rather a teleferic, which was used to train the French Olympic ski team. After adopting Emile Allais' skiing method, the French Olympic team was the best in the world. Allais had become the world champion of downhill skiing in 1937, after earning a bronze medal in the 1936 Winter Olympics. At that time, the top speed was 45 miles per hour—now it is more than 100 miles per hour!

Gilles and I were good skiers, but some of our schoolmates were excellent at it and possible future members of the national skiing team. As a matter of fact, two of them did become members. Unfortunately one of them lost a leg fighting the Germans in 1944.

An arrangement had been made between the high school and the ski lift officials that permitted us to use the teleferic free of charge. However, there was the following specification: we had to use the same console the members of the team were using. Because the team members went down the slope in less than four minutes and each console went up every 15 minutes, that meant we had to go down in less than 10 minutes in order to get on the teleferic in time. Though this required a lot of effort for some of us, we generally managed and had a lot of fun. Years later, Gilles and I could be distinguished from other skiers by the way we slalomed, jumping like tigers on the front ends of our skis just like Emile Allais used to do.

Skiing with the lift was fun, but we enjoyed mountain skiing the best. Climbing in the virgin snow through the forest, looking at animals that were not afraid of us, hearing only the sounds of nature, and forgetting the war was pure joy. I particularly remember a climb that my brother and I made with a friend of ours in the winter of 1943. That particular winter there was a lot of snow in the valley and in the mountains. The three of us decided to climb the mountain in the back of the Le Casset village. In the 1940s, mountain climbing was not only a sport, but also an adventure. Our skis were rather primitive, and we didn't have any fancy ski clothes. The only important part of our equipment was a good pair of mountain shoes and seal skins. The hair of the seal skins gripped the snow and prevented us from slipping backwards. This permitted us to climb slopes of up to a 25 degree angle.

As we reached the first slopes, the sun began to temper the biting cold, warming our skin, our blood, and the air in our lungs. Within 10 minutes we shed our wind-proof jackets. The climbing of this particular mountain took us four hours and we enjoyed every minute. The trees around us were heavily draped with icy snow. At last we left the last thin line of evergreen shrubs behind and emerged on the open slopes of snow. We stopped for a few minutes and looked down at the valley which seemed so far away with the river now only a dark winding line in the distance, and the village looking like a collection of toy houses. Pretty as it was, we were impatient to reach the top, anticipating our descent. The descent was always a few moments of pure delight during which we would demonstrate our skill of turning right or left as the occasion would demand, jumping over something, or coming to a standstill—whatever was best.

Once we reached the top, we saw a storm brewing in the east and thought it prudent to go down immediately. We expected to do this in half an hour or less, but it ended up taking far longer. After a few turns I broke the tip of one my skis. Unfortunately for me, the plastic tips that can slide onto broken skis had not been invented yet, and the only thing I could do was go down on one ski. This, of course, hindered us considerably. Gilles and our friend cussed me profusely because they had to wait for me during our descent. By the time we reached our friend's home in Le Casset, snow was falling heavily but we had made it before the blinding storm struck.

Our friend's mother wanted Gilles and me to dry off and warm up before we made the last leg of our trip, so she invited us into her home. We sat close to the fireplace where large pine logs were burning. After 15 minutes we decided to head back home. The storm was very bad at that point and our friend's mother gave us a small glass of moonshine to keep us warm. This was my first and last glass of moonshine. Its alcohol warmed our bodies and gave us the energy to run. Within 20 minutes we reached our parents' home, where we immediately collapsed in a heap in our common bed due to the effects of fatigue and the brew.

Should Borders Be Respected?

France is divided into departments. Menton and Roquebrune, where I was raised, are both in the Department of Alpes Maritimes. This department is named for the southern part of the Alps, which dominate the region. There is no flat land behind the beaches—you can swim in the morning and ski in the afternoon.

Since we were so close to the border of France and Italy, it was easy to cross over through the mountains, which is where this story comes in. We had a cousin who lived in Monaco who loved to climb mountains like us. One day, when we were teenagers, our cousin decided to climb a nearby mountain and invited my brother and me to join. I cannot remember the name of the mountain, but its summit is at the border of Italy. When we reached the summit, the weather was bad. It was very cold and windy, so my brother and I decided to eat our sandwiches in Italy where the weather was calmer. Our cousin decided to stay on the French side of the border. When we asked him why, he told us he could not go to Italy because he did not have a passport. No comment.

Pure Luck

Lyon is the second most populated city in France, and during World War II, it became the center of the Resistance against the German occupation. In 1943, I was going to Châlons-en-Champagne but had to catch the train in Lyon. Having time before my train, I went to see a film by Jean Renoir. A few hours after I left the cinema, it was blown up—a job carried out by the underground. I never learned why, but I do know that I had been very lucky. I could have been killed.

Cigarette Butts: A Mathematical Problem

During the German and Italian occupation of France (June 1940 - August 1944), the worst problem was the lack of food, especially for children—including teenagers like Gilles and me—who were high school boarders in Briançon at the time. Things improved just a bit for me personally in June 1943, when I turned 18 years old. I was given a tobacco card by the government, which permitted me to buy two packs of French cigarettes, the famous *Gauloises*, every ten days. Since I did not smoke, I exchanged the cigarettes for food with some of my schoolmates whose parents had farms around Briançon. One day I made the bargain of a lifetime: I exchanged one cigarette for one egg, two walnuts, and a piece of ham!

This exchange of cigarettes for food was great for me, but for the real smokers, these years were a nightmare. They were so desperate that they would save cigarette butts to smoke later. They had figured out that if they took the tobacco from three cigarette butts and wrapped it in a thin cigarette paper, they could make one new cigarette. One day, based on this, our mathematics instructor asked us, "How many cigarettes can one make out of 10 cigarette butts?" The mathematical answer is 4 cigarettes with two butts left over. But there is a catch, which leads to the following, very important answer for a true smoker.

Out of nine butts, a smoker can make three cigarettes that he smokes. Now he has three butts, out of which he can make one more cigarette. After smoking that he has one butt, to which he adds the tenth butt. He borrows one more butt from a friend, to make the last cigarette. After smoking it, he gives the resulting newly created butt back to his friend.

Looking for an Honest Man

In 1946, the French people had to vote for the candidates they wanted to represent them in their new government, The Fourth Republic. It was a time of political mistrust and election committees were looking for honest men to help prevent fraud. Although I was barely 21 years old, I was selected to help with the election. I suspect I was chosen was because my father was the vice-mayor of the community. Regardless, that evening I was to look at the ballots. If voters did not like any of the candidates, they could write in a name of their choice. Only one person did, and I recognized the handwriting immediately—it was my mother's.

2

Escaping France and My Time in the Air Force

Questions About the Escape

During our escape from France during World War II, we met a guide that our parents had paid to get us across the Spanish border. This is the story of how we crossed the border with our seemingly lost guide. In order to reach the town of Llívia, a Spanish enclave, we had to take the Little Yellow Train and get off at the Font-Romeu railway station where we met our guide and then walked a few miles to reach the Plateau of Las Puntas. The northern edge the plateau was the border between France and Llívia. The town of Llívia itself was nestled at the bottom of the southern slope of the plateau. We were walking along a dirt road, only a short distance from the French town of Augustine, where we were to leave the road and walk to the left of the plateau away from Augustine. There we met an old Frenchman cleaning the road with a broom. He called to us, "Hey, you boys! If you want to go to Augustine, it is easier to take this shortcut." We told him that we were not going to Augustine, and he quickly guessed that we were attempting to cross the border.He shouted, "Be careful. The Germans are there with dogs today. I usually can see them from here. If you see my broom going back and forth, that means go for it. If you see that I have stopped moving my broom, it means that there is too much danger and you need to go back to the road and try another time."

We waited and when we saw his broom going back and forth, the three of us ran over the plateau. Halfway across, our guide indicated a western direction and told us, "This is the way." I had a gut feeling that she was wrong because she was pointing to rocky ground devoid of trees. It was hard for me to believe that the village was there with no evidence of running water. I told her she was lost. With no time to argue with our guide, I looked around and decided on the spur of the moment that we should go south. There were a few trees on the edge of the plateau, an indication that there might be water around. Gilles, who generally never believed that I could ever be right, believed me this time and left the young woman behind. Running at full speed, we were soon at the edge of the plateau overlooking a small village in the valley. A few hundred yards below the edge, clinging to the hill, were a few houses. When we reached the first house, we went up to it and asked the woman inside if we were in Llívia. She said we were, and we had never felt so relieved.

Our guide had followed us and a few minutes later, the three of us went down the hill to the center of town where we found a small café. Drinking hot coffee, we said goodbye to our guide who was returning to France.

We had never realized how lucky we were to reach Spain until we solved the question of why our guide seemed lost while we crossed the Spanish border. Neither the day we arrived, nor the next did Gilles and I wonder much about why she didn't seem to know the direction to Llívia when we were on the Las Puntas plateau. We had made it and at that time, we didn't care. We simply assumed she was lost. Yet, this assumption was not a valid one. Here was a woman who made her living by smuggling and guiding people across the Spanish border, yet got lost in broad daylight. This did not make sense. The answer came to me years later when Gilles, Mother, and I were sitting in the living room of her home in Berkeley, California. That day we were reminiscing about our escape and I suddenly rejected the idea that our guide had been lost. I was absolutely sure that she was a double agent. She had been paid directly by the underground and indirectly by our parents to guide us over the border. It was not infeasible that she could have also been paid by the Germans to deliver us straight into their hands. My suspicion was never completely confirmed. However, when I visited the Las Puntas plateau 1986, I found the very spot she had pointed us in the false direction of Llívia. Following it, I found myself on the road to Augustine a few feet from a shepherd cabin, the very place where we were told by the old Frenchman with the broom that the German guards and their dogs had been stationed 42 years before. I believe now that our guide had indeed been a double agent, and wonder how many people she handed to the Germans with her fake directions. We have been lucky. Lucky to have knowledge of the topography of mountains gained through our experience in the Alps, to know where villages were located, and to have an excellent inborn sense of direction. We safely crossed the border because it seems that I have a magnet in my brain, similar to pigeons, and also because I did not have blind trust in our mountain guide.

Bullfights in Spain

After we had escaped Vichy France and had finally reached Spain, we had no idea what to do next. We were alone and no one was there to give us advice. Not speaking Spanish or the dialect of the region, we surrendered to the Spanish police who interrogated us in French and put us in jail for the weekend. On Monday we were told that we were going to another jail in the town of Figueras where we would stay for five days. There we shared a cell with two Frenchmen; one was about 50 years old and the other possibly 30. They had escaped from France because the Gestapo had found out that they were part of the resistance. We became friends and the four of us were soon free thanks to the American Red Cross, officially. However, I think it was an agency of the U.S. government that had an arrangement with General Franco. Young men and women who were escapees from all over Europe were to be freed in exchange for 200 pounds of wheat each. This was a nice arrangement for the Spanish people because of the food shortage during World War II. It was also a nice arrangement for the U.S. and its allies because many of these young men, like the Corcos brothers, ended up joining the Allied Forces in North Africa. We were in the hands of the American Red Cross for two weeks in Barcelona before we took the train to Algeciras and a French boat to Casablanca.

But before we took the train and a few days after we left jail, our older French friends called on us. They invited us to see a *corrida de toros* (bullfight). Being on the payroll of the Resistance, they had enough money to enjoy life and spare some on their young friends. We accepted the invitation to what would be our first and last bullfight. The bullfight was at the large bullring at Plaza de las Arenas. There were many people dressed in colorful clothing, shouting, gesticulating, and having a wonderful time.

The matador appeared, dressed in tight, colored pants and a golden shirt. He dedicated the bull that he was going to kill to a beautiful lady as the audience threw all kinds of things into the ring—rice, hats, and even a dead chicken. The matador raised his arms, smiling and showing his appreciation.

Gilles and I knew nothing about bullfights. The following description is what the Spanish audience was expecting of a true-to-form bullfight. A bullfight consists of four parts: the trial, the sentence, the punishment, and finally the execution. During the trial, the bull is teased by the matador and peons. They use a *capote* (cape), which the bull runs into. The way the bull responds to the teasing teaches the matador the nature of that particular bull: how he moves, if he favors either the right or the left side, how he uses his horns. In other words, what the bull does when he charges is of utmost importance to the matador, who is pulled by two contradictory wishes: he does not want to be gored, but at the same time he wants the audience to appreciate his skill and artistry in bullfighting. If the bull responds favorably to the wish of the matador, he is sentenced to die that afternoon in the arena. That is when the punishment starts. It is the role of the *picadors*, towering on their padded horses, to weaken the bull by wounding him with long pics. During this act, the music is playing and the crowd is roaring its approval. Then, the *banderillos* get as close to the bull as they can on foot and plunge their *banderillas* into the back of the bull, weakening him as much as possible.

Then comes the final act, the execution. The matador faces the bull alone. This is what everyone is waiting for; he plays with the *muleta* (a small cape affixed to a stick). For some reason that is not to clear, at least to me, the bull charges the *muleta* and not the man. The matador obviously counts on this, and his skill is to escape just in time from the trajectory of the bull. The man is so sure of himself that after his play with the *muleta* he walks toward the audience with his back to the bull, which he hopes will not move. This shows how courageous the matador is. Now it is time for the killing. The matador hides his sword inside the *muleta*, does a few more tricks with it, and when the beast is at the right time at the right place, the matador executes him by thrusting the sword high up between the shoulders and into the heart. This is the rule. The reason for this rule is that the bull will only lower his head when the matador brings his body within the range of the horns. If done right, the bull staggers a few seconds and then falls dead. The appreciative audience roars its delight and throws more items into the ring while the matador waves to the crowd. During that time, the dead bull is pulled on his side by a team of three powerful panache horses that go around the ring at least once, sometimes twice, and finally exit. If the matador has killed the bull elegantly and skillfully, he is rewarded with the gift of the two ears of the beast. He then shows them to the crowd. He bows and is finally carried out on the shoulders of his friends. And if this is the last bull to be killed, there will be an overflow of men into the ring, who drink and dance to the music of the band.

This is what a bullfight should be if the bull follows the rules and if the matador is a great one. The bullfight can be a display of grace and swordsmanship, or it can be a dull slaughter. That afternoon it was more the latter than the former. The first bull to appear looked shy; he had no pep. He seemed to know what was in store for him, or perhaps he was hurt during the morning run. The crowd shouted its disapproval. The bull was to be led away out of the ring. This was done by bringing steers in and for some reason, the bull followed them. The next morning, as it is customary, he undoubtedly was slaughtered and his meat sold as steaks.

The next bull was more vivacious. He responded with lots of energy to the teasing of the matador. However, he obviously had not read the book on how to be a good bull in the arena, for when the time for the *picador* to weaken the bull; the latter was more concerned with attacking the horse than the man on its back. Soon he was able to pierce the padding of the horse and we saw the bloody guts of the horse as he was lifted by the powerful horns of the bull. Another *picador* had come to finish that part of the bullfight. By that time my interest in bullfighting had decreased to zero. I did not pay much attention as to how that particular bull was killed by the matador, but I guess he must have done all right judging by the reaction of the crowd.

I felt better a few minutes later when another bull came into the ring. He was not as energetic as the previous one. He became weak from the teasing of the *picadors* and the placing of the *banderillas*, for when the time came for the matador to do his thing; the bull did not want to do his. He refused to fight and had to be urged to do so. It ended up looking more like a slaughter than a fight. The audience was screaming at the *picadors*, matador, and the like, throwing hats into the arena. These two final fights were a big disappointment for everyone concerned and the whole show had ended on a sour note. We returned to our quarters with the firm conviction that bullfights were not our cup of tea.

That was not the last we would hear from our French friends. After the France's liberation, the 30-year-old man went to see my parents on the French Riviera to find out what had happened to me and my brother. Father told him that we were in the French Air Force being trained in the United States.

Casablanca

During our service in the Air Force we stayed in Casablanca, Morocco for a while. This was dull because very little happened while we were there. We were simply waiting for our boat to the United States to arrive. However, I do have a few stories to tell of what happened to us in Morocco.

One day Gilles and I went to the United Service Organization (USO) in downtown Casablanca, which was frequented by American, French, and British soldiers from every type of service: Infantry, Air Force, and Navy. The main activities were dancing and eating sandwiches—Gilles and I decided to go for sandwiches. The woman who served us our sandwiches asked us where our home was. The following is the shortest ensuing conversation on record:

> Us: "Antibes."
> The woman: "That is very interesting. My brother lives there."
> Us: "What is his name?"
> The woman: "Pouget. He is a physician."

We were astonished. The woman who had served us the sandwiches was the sister of our home physician. We learned that life is full of surprises. She later invited us to her home where we met her husband who was an intelligence officer. He volunteered to send a radio message to our parents for us. We chose the following words: "Alain-Gilles saw Isabel." Isabel was a Spanish lady who had helped Mother in the summer of 1942. The message meant that we crossed the Spanish border and since it was transmitted through Radio Algiers, our parents would be able to deduce that we were in North Africa. Our parents never heard the message, but friends of theirs heard it, understood it, and told them the good news!

Our parents did not hear from us until two weeks after August 14, 1944, when the Allies landed on the French

Riviera and liberated our hometown. At the time there was no regular mail service between North Africa and France, but planes would fly from Casablanca to Southern France from time to time. One pilot offered to take a delivery of a letters from those of us with parents in France.

Carmen, the Opera

A few weeks after I enlisted in the French Air Force, I had the opportunity to hear the French opera *Carmen,* written by Georges Bizet, in downtown Casablanca. It was the first time I had attended an opera, and I was excited to discover that I enjoyed this type of music. Not all operas of course—my favorites are Italian. However, *Carmen* remains at the top of my favorites list, and I have gone to hear it many times.

The last time I heard *Carmen* was at the Wharton Center at Michigan State University. Unfortunately the singers were from Yugoslavia and their French was unrecognizable. Those of us who knew French were disappointed and left before the end. Nevertheless, *Carmen* still remains my favorite opera, possibly because I went to junior high school with Bizet's grandson. I remember playing marbles with him.

My mother had never been to the opera, but a few years before her death she saw *Carmen* on TV with Placido Domingo as Jose. She liked it.

Rabat

The only Moroccan town we came in contact with other than Casablanca was Rabat, the elegant administrative capital of the

French protectorate. In July 1944, we passed an entire week there. We had left France without finishing our last year of school and had decided we wanted to officially graduate from high school. So, as a condition of our enlistment in the Air Force, we stipulated that we would have a leave of absence to pass the *baccalaureate*. The Air Force presented no objection to our project—at the time there was a shortage of officers, and the Air Force had already classified me and Gilles as officer cadets from the first day of our enlistment, anticipating our high school graduation. We passed the written and oral examinations with flying colors. It did cross our minds that there might have been some bias in our favor in the minds of the examiners. After all we were the only school graduates in uniform and had only recently escaped from France. These were not ordinary circumstances under which to pass an exam.

We had to wait until October 1944, to learn that we could finally go to the United States. We were to take a boat across the ocean out of Oran, Algeria. Once we arrived in Oran, we had to wait two weeks before we were finally on our way. It took us eleven days to cross the Atlantic—a long time. This was because we were protected by destroyers that zigzagged back and forth in front of us. It was a long trip, but we were happy and ate fantastic meals the entire way—I gained a pound a day.

How Many Air Force Wings Can You Wear on Your Chest?

In November 1944, we arrived in the United States to be

trained as pilots. Once trained successfully, we were expected to wear the American wings and the French wings. Some could even wear the Royal Air Force wings as well if they had been pilots in England. One of our peers told us that he could wear a fourth one, but refused to because it was the German wings. This is his story.

He was an Alsatian, which are the German-speaking people of the present-day French region of Alsace. Alsace and Lorraine are two provinces which have taken turns being located either in France or Germany over the years, depending on who had won the previous war. In 1940, France lost the war and so Alsace was part of Germany. This meant that our friend was drafted into the German Air Force as a student pilot. The day he became solo (meaning he could fly the plane alone), he decided to fly to London knowing perfectly well that he might be shot down by the British. He ended up being lucky. When he was over England, he started to yell in French that he was French and wanted to land his plane. He was permitted to safely land his German plane. We were all impressed by his story, but concluded that to do what he did, you would have to be completely crazy, 18-years-old, or both!

A Mystery About Immigration

Twice after World War II, we were informed that we were heirs to some relatives. Through the process of getting our estates though, we discovered something strange. It turned out that there was no official record of us being soldiers in the U.S. in 1944. According to the U.S. government, we had come to the United States in 1947. However, some states like New York and Alabama had records of us being in the U.S. earlier, due to marriage licenses filed with American girls. I have only recently discovered the reason for this discrepancy. It turns out that we had never officially crossed the U.S. border in 1944 because the border guard did not have the right to ask people in uniform where they were coming from.

Selma, Alabama

On November 4, 1944, as members of the French Air Force, we went directly by train from New York to Craig Air Force Base, which was a bit north of Selma, Alabama. There we were isolated for two weeks to ensure we had not brought over any tropical diseases. Finally, we were told that we could leave the base and my brother and I decided to go see a movie in Selma. Although we had heard about racism in the United States, we were not ready to discover the segregation black Americans faced. Gilles and I, not knowing the local customs, tried to enter the cinema but were informed that we were using the wrong entrance. We had tried to walk through the entrance for "colored people," and were told to enter through the "white entrance" instead because we belonged to the master race. This was news to us.

There is a myth among black people in the U.S. that racism does not exist in France. It does, but it is not as powerful as it is in the U.S. Most black people live outside of France in what used to be the French colonies, and were never French citizens. The problem of racism is therefore different in those countries. Today the victims of racism in France are mostly Arabs.

Some People in Louisiana Speak French

While in the Air Force, I remember a trip I took to New Orleans, Louisiana. I had wanted to visit New Orleans because of its French past. I was not alone in this wish, so I and the other French Air Force cadets decided to take the bus from Biloxi, Mississippi, to New Orleans. We were speaking French and hadn't realized that some people would be able to understand us. A young lady had her leg over the wheel well of the bus and one of my traveling partners said, "Oh, quelle belle jambe!" or "Oh, what a beautiful leg!" Next to the young lady was her mother who said, "thank you," to the young man. The young man said, "Forgive me," to which the mother said, "No problem, it was a cry of admiration."

Once we arrived in New Orleans that same day, we met a man who spoke to us in French about the Louisiana Purchase. I believe that he was half drunk, but he told us that he thought it was the best real estate deal that the U.S. had ever made. In return for $15 million, the U.S. nominally acquired a total of 828,000 square miles, out of which 10 states were carved.

Years later I went back to New Orleans with my wife. We were in the French Quarter at noon and decided to eat lunch in a restaurant. We found one with an excellent meal and a waitress that spoke French. I hadn't paid much attention to the name of the restaurant until we were home again and I decided to look it up. It was *Antoine,* which was one of the best French restaurants in Louisiana, possibly in the U.S.

French Canadians Speak a Strange French

When the war was over, we were to head back to France. However, it took a while before we could get a ship so we were sent to an airbase called Selfridge Field, north of Detroit, Michigan to wait. At the time, crossing the border into Canada was very simple for those in uniform: we simply crossed the bridge. So some of us decided to visit Windsor in Canada, where we saw signs in French. One of them was funny to us. It read, *DEFENSE DE TREPASSER*, which in English translates to DO NOT TRESPASS. The problem is that the meaning of *trespasser* has changed in the last 300 years. *Trespasser* in modern French means "to die." So the comical sign was telling us, DO NOT DIE. We had no intention of doing that!

The Handkerchief

Once back at home, I took the late afternoon train to Biarritz, France. Next to me was a young lady who was obviously tired. She began falling asleep, and as she did, her head fell on my shoulder. Across from us was anolder couple who turned out to be her grandparents. Seeing us, her grandma smiled. When the young lady woke up a bit, I asked her grandma if she had met her husband that way or if she dropped her handkerchief as was the custom in France years ago. She answered, "Idon't remember, but I got him." I did not get the young lady, but maybe I should have tried, because she was very pretty.

This custom reminds me of a story about Bernard Le Bouvier de Fontenelle who was secretary of the Academy of Sciences for 50 years. When he was 90, a woman dropped her handkerchief, and Fontenelle tried to pick it up but could not. Supposedly, he said, "One is not always 80 years old."- Fontenellle's joke is that the true expression is, "One is not always twenty years old."

3

College in the States

Boxing Match?

On my way to attend college in California in 1947, I stopped in New York to see a woman named Martha. She had taken care of my brother and me when we were kids in France while our mother was helping our father with his business. The date of my visit was December 5, 1947, which was a famous day in boxing because of a match between Joe Louis and Joe Walcott. We decided to watch the match during my visit, so Martha's husband turned on the television and went to the kitchen to get some beer. By the time he came back to the living room, the match was over! Walcott had knocked out Louis in the first round or was it the reverse.

Baseball, Anyone?

I started my college life at California Polytechnic College at San Luis Obispo. One day I was on campus when most students had gone home—I believe it was Thanksgiving. As I was walking on campus, I heard someone yell, "Hey, Frenchie, do you want to play baseball?" I looked over to see the group playing baseball was obviously short of players. I had never played baseball before, because it is not a known sport in France. However, I accepted and I was given a bat. I hit the ball far away and heard, "Frenchie, go home!" Not knowing what that meant, I picked up my sweater and went home. Since then, I found out that I need a dictionary to understand baseball talk.

An Incredible Story

The most astonishing story that happened to me is the following. I was studying horticulture in San Luis Obispo, California in 1947. One evening I was eating in the dormitory cafeteria, when a man in his mid-20s sat down next to me. After a few moments, he asked me where in France I was from.

"The French Riviera," I replied.

"Which part of the French Riviera?" He asked.

"Near Nice," I said, thinking he was just kindly making small talk.

"Where near Nice?"

"Menton," I replied.

"What part of Menton?" He pressed.

"Wait a minute. Have you been to Menton?" I asked incredulously.

"Yes, we liberated the town. We stayed a few days."

"Where did you sleep?" I asked.

"In tents, next to a small river."

He went on to describe the river at the bottom of the hill where my parents had a flower farm.

There I was, thousands of miles from the French Riviera, and someone I was eating with had liberated my hometown two years before. He was one of the Nisei (a person born in America but whose parents are immigrants from Japan) who volunteered to serve during World War II. I owe a debt of gratitude to him and his comrades for liberating my hometown.

Fire in Santa Barbara County

One year while I was at San Luis Obispo, it was Christmas vacation and the only students on campus were foreign students like me. We got a call from the fire department that there was a fire in the Santa Barbara forest and they needed volunteers to fight the fire. Some of us volunteered. As soon as we arrived, a cook asked us where we came from. When it was my turn, I told him I was French. Immediately he declared that I was going to be his helper—assuming that if I were French, I must know how to cook steaks and make very good sandwiches. I did not tell him that that was certainly not the case. I cooked for 23 hours and never saw the fire, but I got paid $23 for my work. My fellow foreign friends fought the fire with shovels for 12 hours and earned only $12 for their work. What kind of justice is that?

I Am a Mason

One Sunday, I was on the campus of the California Polytechnic College watering pots in one of the department of horticulture's greenhouses, when the phone rang. It was a man who was looking for someone who knew how to build a rock wall in his garden without using cement. I answered that I knew one—me! I had learned this trade when I was a teenager on the French Riviera. He came right away and picked me up. I found stones and a few tools including a hammer. I built his wall in seven hours. The man was so happy that he paid me $3 an hour and gave me a bottle of wine. I was also happy because the minimum wage at the time was 60 cents. That evening I went dancing.

The Birth of Michigan State University

In 1950, I moved from San Luis Obispo, California, to East Lansing, Michigan to continue my studies. Five years later, 1955, was a very important year for the institution of higher learning in East Lansing, Michigan. The college there changed its name from Michigan State College to Michigan State University. It was also the year that the American Institute of Biological Sciences (AIBS) decided to hold its annual meeting in East Lansing. I never forgot two of the speakers who had a great sense of humor, C.C. Li and Paul Anderson.

Dr. Li told us that a year before, Professor Sewall Wright—a population geneticist—was asked to explain his work at the annual meeting, but no one understood his lecture (a genius should never be asked to explain his or her work). So this time, said Dr. Li, the AIBS asked a half-genius to explain the genius's contribution to science. Of course that was Dr. Li, whose lecture was much better understood than Dr. Wright's.

The other joker was Professor Anderson, a famous botanist who told us that he was raised in East Lansing and had worked in the Beal Garden to earn money. Then he added—and this is one of the best jokes I ever heard—"I have worked here so long, the people I have known have become buildings." What was true for Professor Anderson then is also true for me now. I knew President Hannah before he became the administration building and I knew Professor Bessey before he became a teaching building.

Two Steel Bars

Ph.D. candidates have to pass a preliminary oral exam where they are asked to answer any question brought up by the committee reviewing them. According to my brother, one year at the University of Michigan, the physics Ph.D. candidates were asked, "If you have two steel bars and a ruler, and one of the bars is a magnet, which one of the steel bars is the magnet?" I am not a physicist, but when my brother asked me that question, it took me 15 minutes to get the correct answer. The Ph.D. candidates had 20 minutes to answer, and eight of them flunked. The question had to do with imagination. If you cannot apply a principle that you've learned to a situation, you are not fit to do research.

One summer day when I was getting my Ph.D. in plant breeding, I was weeding some experimental corn plants with two high school students. I asked them the question about the steel bars. One of them gave me the answer within one minute, and I was impressed. A few months later I happened to see the other student in downtown Lansing and I asked him what happened to his friend. He told me that he was at MIT after receiving a four-year scholarship. No wonder he knew about magnetism.[3]

---

3   To find the answer to this question, you can look to a picture of a magnet in any physics book or on the internet.

Kids Often Learn by Themselves

In 1950, I was attending college and living in what we called the G.I.barracks on the campus of Michigan State University. One of my neighbors had a little boy who went with him to watch basketball games. Soon the kid learned how to count 2,4,6,8... instead of 1,2,3,4...

Here is another story. I had a friend who was a psychologist. He and his family moved to the state of Washington where it was possible for children to attend school before the age of 5, but had to first be examined by a psychologist to see if they were ready for schooling. My friend was to evaluate a little boy who was four. He had been adopted by a couple whose home had no books, and only the Sunday newspaper to read. The kid always had his nose in the comics, acting like he was reading them. His mother was smart enough to figure that her son was somebody special and that maybe he should start school early. My friend confirmed that the boy was not only ready, but had the maturity of a third grader. I wish I knew what became of him.

Touch Down

It was also in 1955 that one of the most important football games between Notre Dame and Michigan State was played. People drove in from all over in all types of cars, including Cadillacs, to attend. There was a shortage of parking for the event and so those of us living on campus in the G.I. barracks came up with the idea of renting the spaces between the barracks for $1 each. We told the renters that we would take good care of their cars for that price and everything went smoothly.

That afternoon as I went to do some research—I was a graduate student at the time—I was stopped three times by ticket scalpers who asked if I had a ticket to see the big game. They were ready to pay me $50 for it! Unfortunately I did not have any tickets to sell, which was too bad because for $50 I could have fed my family for two weeks. As I approached the stadium, a French friend of mine who was a gate keeper for the afternoon game asked me if I wanted to go inside to watch the game. If yes, he would let me in for nothing. I told him I was not interested. As a matter of fact, I never went to a single football game. I do not understand what is so thrilling about players of one team knocking down players of another team. The game is so physically dangerous and many players get hurt.

4

Adulthood

Breakfast, Anyone?

Not everyone gets the chance to have breakfast with a former vice-president of the United States, but I was lucky enough to get that opportunity while getting my Ph.D. in corn breeding. I was invited to have breakfast with Henry Wallace, the vice-president under President Franklin D. Roosevelt. Wallace was also the president of the Pioneer corn seed company. During the breakfast we talked about corn. I wished we had talked about politics—I might have learned something.

Stories About American Dentists

My first job after I received my Ph.D. in corn breeding was in peach breeding. For this particular job I moved from East Lansing, Michigan to the small town of Red Bluff in Northern California where there was only one dentist. Unfortunately tragedy struck: the dentist and his son died while hiking in Lassen Park, which is very close to Red Bluff. Fortunately for the citizens of Red Bluff, there was no problem finding another dentist who had recently been discharged from the Air Force. He had a good sense of humor and told me this story.

There were two friends in the Air Force. One was a dentist and the other was a pilot. They were both discharged, and a few months later, the pilot went to have his teeth checked by his friend, the dentist. The dentist told him he had some cavities. "How come?" asked the pilot. "You just checked my teeth not too long ago."

The dentist answered, "You cannot trust an Air Force dentist."

After Red Bluff, my family moved to Santa Barbara where I had my teeth checked by a dentist who was very skillful. I congratulated him on his trade, and he told me that if he were not skillful, he could not have been a dentist. He said he would have been kicked out of the school of dentistry— it had even happened to someone he knew. I asked him what happened to his unlucky friend. His answer: "He became a physician."

Looking for a Bug

As I mentioned, after getting my Ph.D., my first job was in peach breeding. This was alright for about two years until my boss went bankrupt and told me he could not afford to pay me anymore. I had to find another job, which I found out was not an easy task. I was told that I was overeducated for most jobs that were available. Fortunately my first wife was teaching French at the local high school, which allowed us to still eat.

I found temporary work as a substitute math teacher at the high school one month and another month I joined a USDA employee in search of a wheat pest that we were hoping never to find. One day on the job, I went to a farm and introduced myself to the owner. The first thing he asked me was "are you with the sheriff's department?" When I told him I was not, he relaxed, and I soon found out why. Besides farming, he was also breeding fighting cocks, which I saw in cages around the property. There was something else something strange about him, too. He was speaking what I would consider to be the King's English. When I asked him where he learned to breed cocks, he told me nowhere, but that he had taken a course in genetics when he was majoring in English at Michigan State University. He had answered my questions, so I went looking for the bug.

Math Substitute Teacher

When I was a substitute math teacher at Red Bluff High School in Northern California, I used the following story to teach students that mathematics has drawbacks. Drawbacks are when fractions of an odd number, such as 17, never total whole unit. My students were impressed because no one had ever illustrated the nature of mathematics with stories before.

Among my parents' friends there was a painter, whom everyone including his wife called Vanden (his real name was too long for anyone to remember). He would often come through the hills from his house in the old village of Roque-brune to paint the flowers in our garden (he was particularly fond of roses). He even painted our mother once—that painting, among others that he gave or sold to our parents— Gilles and I still have. As Vanden was an excellent conversationalist, our parents enjoyed having him for lunch or tea when he would visit. One story that always impressed me was the following:

Many years ago there was an old Arab who had three sons. When he died, he left a will in which he gave half his estate to his eldest son, one third to his second son, and one ninth to his third son. His estate consisted of 17 mules. As soon as he left this earth, his three sons started fighting because they all wanted more than their share. His eldest son wanted 9 mules, his second son wanted six mules, and his youngest wanted two mules. After finding out that it was impossible to divide 17 mules according to their father's wishes, they called on a *cadi* (judge) to solve this touchy problem. The *cadi* thought for a while (the reader can do the same). After half an hour the *cadi* called his attendant, "Mohamed, go to the barn and get my mule." As soon as the mule was there, he started to distribute the estate. He gave 9 mules to the eldest son, six mules to the second son, and two mules to the third. Then he said, "Mohamed, bring back my mule to the stable."

The Cadillac

Still looking for a permanent job in the summer of 1960, I found another tentative job working for the California department of agriculture as a plant pathologist. We were looking for viruses that attack stone fruits. One day four of us stopped to eat at a restaurant when we suddenly heard a car crash. We ran out to see if anyone needed help. There were two cars: one was a state car like ours with a driver who said he was alright. The driver of the other car took off, but that was not the end of the story. It turned out that we were the only witnesses. When we got back to our office, the police were already there waiting to ask us questions. Among the questions was what kind of car had hit the state car? We all said it was a Cadillac. The next question was, what color was it? To our astonishment, we each came up with four different answers; however, the police were not surprised. They told us that it's common for witnesses to disagree about details of what they saw, and it doesn't necessarily mean they're lying. I find this very interesting. Still, the story did not end there. Two years later a lawyer phoned me and asked me similar questions about the crash. I asked him if I was going to be a witness in court, and he said no. That was fine with me!

A Clot

My father was in World War I, and unlike others he was not wounded in the war, but he was poisoned by drinking contaminated water. After he was poisoned, his kidneys were affected and he suffered from this affliction the rest of his life. He should have died early from kidney disease, but instead he died of a clot in his heart at the age of 76 in San Francisco, California.

After the funeral, we went home and our mother told us to immediately rearrange our father's bedroom to put another bed in it. We did not understand the urgency until she explained that for the last ten years of our father's life, she had taken care of him—not knowing if he was going to die each night. She was exhausted and changing our father's bedroom into her granddaughter's bedroom was like turning to a new chapter of her life.

She was not the only woman I knew who did this. Years later, the wife of one of my best friends also rearranged the furniture after he had been moved to a home. She was exhausted after taking care of him for 5 years after he had a stroke that paralyzed the right side of his body. She and my mother both loved their husbands dearly, but there was a limit to what they could do both physically and mentally. They had to think about themselves, lest they become victims of their past.

Artichoke

In addition to growing carnations on the French Riviera, we also grew artichokes. They were always the first vegetable of the season. However, during the summer months, the artichokes would be abundant and tasty, but very small and not worth gathering to sell. Only the growers and their neighbors knew to collect and eat them. The recipe is very simple: boil the artichokes whole and then serve with lettuce and peas to enjoy.

Years later, I went to see the maritime museum in Monterey, California, and on my way I saw fields of artichokes. It was August and they were in bloom.[4] So, on my way back to San Francisco, I stopped and picked up a large bag to fill up with the small artichokes. There was nobody around, but there was a sign that read, "A DOLLLAR A BAG." People were honest; there was money in a basket. I was so happy with my purchase that I brought the artichokes to my mother who cooked for us.

---

4   What you eat are the flowers of the artichokes. Most people in the United States do not eat fresh artichokes. They only know the canned variety. I have taught a few of them how to eat them.

A Move to Monmouth, Oregon

My family and I moved from Santa Barbara to Monmouth, Oregon in September 1963. I had accepted an instructorship at the College of Education (now Western Oregon University). The town was very small with one traffic light, a grocery store—that looked more like a museum—and a pharmacy.

The first problem we encountered was finding a house. My wife, a city girl, did not like living in such a small town like Monmouth, so we started our search for a house 15 miles from Monmouth, in Salem. This leads me to the next story.

After seeing two or three houses for sale, we found one that we liked. Unfortunately, the real estate agent told us that we would like living there because it was a racially restricted area. Since I did not want to live in such an area—I like human diversity—we left and went back to our motel room. Half an hour later, someone knocked at the door. It was our real estate agent accompanied by his wife who wanted to know why we did not pursue the house. She told us that her husband was new at this job. I gave her our reason and told her I hoped that he was more successful the next time.

Later that day, we decided to go to Monmouth and look for a house there. Next to the college campus, we saw new houses that were in all different stages of being built. We were attracted to one and asked a man with a ladder how we could get in touch with the real estate agency. He said that he was the builder and he would happily sell one of the houses to us. After asking if I was on the college faculty, he advised me to buy a specific house because it had beautiful book shelves, a Franklin stove, and could not be closer to campus. Only a small fence separated the backyard from the campus grounds. I told the builder I wanted to buy the house. We shook hands and arranged to meet on Monday morning. I called the moving company to have my furniture delivered at 8 a.m. that morning. When I arrived at the house I was pleased to find the van right on time in front of the house, and the builder was there too.

A few minutes later, a woman arrived and asked us what we were doing in front of her house and claimed that she had bought it over the weekend. Unfortunately, she had bought the house from the salesman working for the builder, and there had been no communication between the two about my previous arrangement. The builder insisted that I had bought the house first and being the boss, his judgment prevailed. The woman left furious. I was left wondering why the builder had taken my side so vigorously. He told me without my asking: if he sold the house to me he did not have to pay his salesman a $1,000 commission.

———————

I have said that Monmouth was a small town, but I realized how small it really was when one day I was lecturing and I heard the sound of a siren outside. One student left immediately, telling me that he had to go because he was the ambulance driver. He returned twenty minutes later.

Solitude

I do not play any part in this story, but I thought that I should include it in this book. When I was teaching in Oregon, a colleague told me about an adventure that he and his son had driving in southeastern Oregon where very few people lived. They came to a sign that said, DETOUR, and decided to take it. It was a very narrow road that led to a farm. When they arrived, the farmer came out smiling and admitted that he had put out the DETOUR sign because he was lonely and needed someone to talk to. He fed them and after two hours they took the narrow road back to where the sign was.

A Building in East Berlin[5]

The most incredible story that happened to my brother and me is the following. After World War I, Germany was in deep trouble; the country was supposed to pay a large sum of money in reparations to the Allies for losing the war. Due to this, the German currency became worthless and foreigners could buy things very inexpensively. One of my uncles bought real estate in Berlin and rented it out to tenants. Unfortunately, when Hitler came to power in 1933, he could no longer export the money he was making off the tenants to France and could only spend it in Germany. His bad luck continued when he was unable collect rent during the Second World War After the war, the country split. Although he was lucky that his real estate was not destroyed by the bombings,

---

5   I have written this story in detail in my book, *Four True Stories of a French Family.*

it was located in East Germany. This of course meant that my uncle could still not collect the rent because East Germany was communist.

My uncle died in 1959 as a wealthy man with no children. His fortune was distributed as such in his will: 10% to my father, 3% to each of his nephews, and the rest to charities. My father died 3 months after his brother, and my mother became the executor of both estates. It took a lot of time and patience on her part to sort everything out because my uncle's will was far from perfect. Plus, there was the issue of his real estate being in East Germany under a communist government. There was nothing my mother could do at the time, and we all ended up forgetting about it until 1990, when the famous Berlin Wall fell. At that time, I received a notice that the new German government was looking for the owners or heirs of the properties in East Germany. The notice was from French lawyers who specialized in this type of work. This was the beginning of our adventure.

Upon learning more about the property, we discovered that when my uncle had said that it was just two little houses, he was wrong. It was actually a whole building with 17 apartments. I suppose that when my uncle wrote his will, he may have had dementia. Next, we discovered that his will was valid only in East Germany and not valid in West Germany because it had been more than 25 years since his death. It got complicated and the French lawyers quit working for us. Then in 2004, a lawyer from East Germany wrote to me, saying he was going to solve the problem—and he did! The city of Berlin bought the building for $650,000 and my brother and I finally received our $25,000 dollars instead of the $250,000 if the will had not been recognized. In 1995, the last Russians left East Germany and we learned that the Corcos building had been the headquarters of a section of the Russian army. After their departure, nothing was left in the inside. Only the walls of the building remained.[6]

A Return to the French Riviera

People in Southern France are known to be more relaxed than the Parisians who live a fast life—always hurrying someplace or another. That was true at least until the 1960s when I went back to France after the death of my father. I wanted to take a sentimental journey to see the Riviera. That particular day, I was in Cannes and wanted to have my hair cut so I went into a barbershop at 9 a.m. As I entered, the barber told me he could not cut my hair because he was going to the market to get some food. Obviously he knew what was important.

While visiting Cannes, I was also looking for a friend who lived there. I was not very familiar with the area and did not know the address, so I asked someone on the street for help. I was told to turn right and then left. *If I see a big tree*, I went too far. That italicized expression is always part of the explanation of how to get from here to there given by a citizen of the French Riviera. Later, I took a taxi, and the friendly driver told me that I was his last client for the morning. He was going to take his siesta. All of these interactions made me

---

6   I wrote the story of the Corcos building in my book.

happy—turns out nothing had changed on the Riviera. It was just the same as when I had left it thirteen years before.

An Eel Story

In the summer of 1965, I was on vacation in France with my first wife who was also French. She had partially grown up in the little town of Margaux, which is well known for its wine. During this trip I met her family, including her sister, Janine, and her brother-in-law, Pierre. Pierre was a very good hunter and fisherman. One day he asked if I wanted to accompany him to fish for eels. I learned that you cannot fish for eels whenever you like because eels have special habits—they go up the Garonne River with the tides. To fish eels you need a rod, string, worms, and a net to hold out and catch the eels as they jump out of the water to get the worm. That particular day, I caught nine eels and Pierre caught 50! We went happily home where Pierre cooked the eels over a fire. I had never eaten eels before, but discovered that they taste like tuna.

A Wine Story

I always wanted to know if the French people knew their wines, and while visiting my wife's family in Margaux in 1970, I had the chance to find out. That particular day the whole family had gone shopping in Bordeaux, leaving me alone and ready to do a very important scientific experiment. I switched two types of wines from their bottles. I put the best wine in the ordinary wine bottle and ordinary wine in the best wine bottle. Then, I waited for the family to return.

It took my sister-in-law less than two minutes to determine that a criminal had switched the wines and that the criminal was me! I later found out that the family still talks about my crude experiment to this day. Well, I guess my hypothesis was correct—some people in France do know their wines.

The Greek Interpreters

In 1973, I joined a local Sherlock Holmes club called The Greek Interpreters. There I met a professor of criminal justice whose specialty was fingerprints. We became friends and one day he came to my office to use my dissecting scope—why he did not have one of his own is a mystery. In any case, he wanted to inspect a bullet, and not just any bullet, but the one that killed Robert F. Kennedy. He did not find anything to suggest that the killer, Sirhan Bishara Sirhan, had an accomplice—a mystery we still do not have an answer to.

A Cave

Our parents sold their property, *Clair Matin,* in 1950 because my brother Gilles and I had decided to stay in the United States. In 1958, an archaeological site was discovered in Roquebrune-Cap-Martin after a few days of torrential rains. Due to the rain, the side of a hill slid down, uncovering the entrance of a cave. Stone tools were found at the site and dated to be between 1 million and 1.05 million years old, making it one of the earliest sites of human settlement known in Europe.

The discovery of a cave is always interesting, but the

reason for its mention here is because of its location. It was only a few hundred feet from our property at the bottom of the hill. I visited Roquebrune in 1978, but I regret not going to see the cave.

Early Romance?

In 1978, my second wife Joanne (an American) and I took a trip to see where I was raised on the French Riviera. This trip brought this astonishing story.

After seeing my childhood home, *Clair Matin*, Joanne was hungry. We descended the 99 steps that led us to Carnolès, a small suburb of Menton, but is administratively part of the township of Roquebrune-Cap-Martin. Walking along the main street, we found a nice looking restaurant with a woman standing out front. I asked her if it was a good restaurant, and she answered that it was hers. So we went in and she asked us what we wanted to eat. I translated the question for Joanne. Immediately the owner of the restaurant asked me why I was speaking English to my wife. I answered that she did not speak a word of French and that we were Americans. The lady told me that I could not be, because my French accent was just like hers—from the region we were in. She asked me who I was, and this is the conversation we had:

Me: Did you hear about the Corcos family who lived up the hill years ago?
She: Are you Gilles or Alain?
Me: Alain.

She: What happened to Gilles?

Me: He is also living in the United States where he is a professor of engineering.

She: This does not astonish me. He was so smart! He helped me do my homework when we were in grammar school.

Here in a small restaurant on the French Riviera I had discovered my brother's first girlfriend; a romance that happened more than 50 years before.

Stolen Land

My brother Gilles adopted a Native American girl when she was born. When she grew up, she got married and had two boys. In school, one of the boys had learned how badly the Native Americans were by treated by the "white" people. When he got home from school that day, he asked his father (of British origin), "Why did you steal my land?"

A Trip to Remember

My brother and I had a cousin named Francis whom we considered to be our third brother. He joined our family in 1942 when his mother became a victim of the Holocaust (he had never known his father). Being only a few months younger than me, we were in the same classes at the local high school. He grew up to become a famous electrical l engineer.

After 25 years of marriage, he and his wife asked if my wife and I wanted to visit the Canadian Rocky Mountains together.

It was fantastic trip not only because we were together, but because we also saw many beautiful landscapes. It took us 13 days to go from Lansing, Michigan to San Francisco, California. Our conversations were mostly in English because my American wife did not speak a word of French. Fortunately, Colette, Francis's wife, was an English teacher and Francis also spoke English (with a French accent). He could even say funny jokes in English. For instance, one morning we went to eat breakfast in a restaurant and the waitress asked Francis what he wanted to eat. He answered, "Two eggs any style." The waitress did not understand the joke and tried to explain what any style meant. Francis insisted that since the words "any style" were on the menu he wanted two eggs any style. Finally he told the waitress to bring him two boiled eggs.

Who Was He?

I used to subscribe to *Business Week* magazine. On the cover of one issue there was a picture of a young Frenchman who had done something special after getting his master's degree from Yale—I don't remember what.

However, I was struck by the picture because the young man resembled one of my cousins, Daniel. He even had the same family name—Jouve. The resemblance was so striking that my mother insisted that it was my cousin. He was not of course, but there must have been some familial link between them. Our Daniel had been adopted by one of my uncles and his wife. We had a suspicion that he was a nephew of my aunt. I asked my mother if my aunt had a younger brother who could have been the father of Daniel and of the young man on the *Business Week* cover. My mother did not know and my hypothesis was never verified, but it makes sense to me. In both France and the United States there have been cases of adoption similar to that of Daniel.

We Could Have Died

My mother died in November of 1980, so on Christmas Eve, my wife Joanne and I had driven to Berkeley, California for her memorial. While we were there, I collected some of the things that reminded me of our past together, including paintings. The trunk and backseat of our car were full as we took off for home in Michigan. The trip was fine until we reached Illinois.

We had slept in a motel for the night and had no idea that it had rained earlier in the morning and that all that rain had turned into ice. After a few miles on the freeway, we hit a lake of ice and the car spun around in circle before landing in a ditch, with the front facing the freeway. Looking around we saw many cars flying off the freeway like ours did. My wife said, "What are we going to do? We need help." We had no cell phone as those had not been not invented yet. It looked like we were stuck for a while.

After a few minutes, I decided to investigate where we had landed. I opened the door and found that the ground under the car was full of little rocks and was not at all icy. I told my wife we might get out of the ditch by creeping out in first gear. She tried, and very slowly we were back on the freeway. Until we reached Indiana, Joanne drove the car at fifteen miles per hour. The roads in Indiana were better than in Illinois, and Joanne was able to resume a normal speed. We reached home about one and half hours later than expected.

Progress in Surgery

I had to have hip surgery in 1982. Afterwards, I stayed in the hospital for five days and had to attend physical therapy for two weeks once back home. In 2021, my son had hip surgery, but he came back from the hospital the same day he was operated on, and within a few days, he was walking normally. No one could ask for better recovery!

In 1982, the retina of my right eye was torn and then repaired with a new tool at the time, called a laser. I never forgot that the distance between the laser light and my eye was measured in feet. Forty years later, the surgery has advanced so much that the distance is now in inches.

A Return to the Alps

In the summer of 1984, my American wife, Joanne, and I were traveling by car from Grenoble to Aix-en-Provence and stopped in the village of Le Monêtier. I wanted to see the Alpine village where Gilles and I had spent our weekends during 1943 and early 1944 meeting our parents, who had taken refuge there from the Nazis. I have fond memories of this village—it was there that we were fed for the week, as there was so little food in the high school cafeteria. Despite warlike conditions, we had a lot of fun skiing.

We parked the car next to the old church, and Joanne and I went to find the two ladies who were dear to my heart: Madame Robert and Madame Rousset, both in their seventies at the time. I will always be grateful to Madame Robert for the many meals she fed us between 1942 and 1944. Her *gratin dauphinois* with all the trimmings is still present in the forefront of my memory. She was happy to see me after so many years. We talked to her for a while and then went to see if Madame Rousset was home. Madame Rousset was the wife of Robert Rousset, who had taught me and my brother to climb mountains. We found her physically fit and mentally alert. Before my wife and I left the village I promised Madame Rousset that I would come back to capture her memories of the events before and during the liberation of the region on tape. I made good on my promise when I came back two years later in 1986. The following are stories she told me during three summer days we passed with her and her sister, Fernande.

To appreciate Madame Rousset's stories, I would like to recap the history of Briançon and its surroundings under the Axis occupation. Briançon was occupied by the Italians on November 11, 1942, two days after American troops landed in North Africa. The French military resistance was soon born, and by March 1943 the first *maquis*, or hidden camps of the free fighting French force, were established in the mountains of La Croix Haute. Robert Rousset and his wife were part of the Briançon *maquis*.

Here is the first story. MR is Madame Rousset and AC is the author, Alain Corcos.

MR: From time to time it was necessary to find out whether the Germans were in the Valleys of La Guisane and La Romanche and if they were, what they were up to. This was a job well suited for a friend of ours who was an officer of The Secret Army and a civil engineer. His formal duty was to periodically check the local roads for safety.

One day, as he was at the base of the Galibier Pass, he was arrested by a German patrol whose chief officer rightly assumed that he was a member of the Resistance. It was decided that he was to be executed as soon as possible. Along with some other Frenchmen, our friend was led to the edge of a rocky precipice. From across the road, German soldiers were given the order to shoot them. At this precise moment an incredible thought went through the mind of our friend: "As long as I am to be killed this way, I might as well try something to save my life, however improbable this might be." As the Germans were aiming, he bent backwards within a second and made a looping (Madame Rousset used the English word "looping") and fell down on the rocks below. He was never hit by a bullet, but he said he psychosomatically felt them pierce through his body.

Though not having been hit by any bullets, he was still bleeding profusely from the cuts and bruises that resulted from his fall against the rocks. The Germans thought they had killed him on the spot and never checked to see if he was really dead. Our friend lay down at the bottom of the precipice for at least two hours. He then stayed at Galibier Pass for two days to recuperate from his wounds and shock.

He drank some water from the river, but had nothing to eat. On the evening of the second day, he went down to the valley and was soon on the threshold of our home where we saw him coming toward us, looking haggard. He said to Robert: "Touch me Rousset, touch me. Am I alive or dead? Am I dreaming?" When he told us his story, we easily understood why the poor man was so disturbed.

In order to take care of his wounds, we undressed him. His shoulders were a mess. They were red and terribly scratched.

AC: Had he a fever?

MR: Not really. He was in a very bad shape but he was alive, which was the important thing. We gave him drink and food. Somewhere, it was written that it was too early for him to die.

AC: He was a fast thinker and courageous man. Is he still alive?

MR: Oh yes. I learned that he is now retired.

AC: You promised to tell me another story about what happened to your husband when he was up the mountains one day.

MR: Oh yes. One day in the summer of 1944, Robert decided to see what was happening on the north side of the Galibier Pass. He climbed the pass and started going down through some pasture lands dotted with old chalets. No one was around, for the region had become a small battlefield between the Germans and the FFI. As Robert was inside one of these chalets looking through his field glasses, he heard a terrible commotion as if someone had jumped onto the corrugated iron roof. This would have been an easy thing for anyone to do because of the steepness of the hillside. Robert, who obviously could not see who jumped on the roof, had only one thought: "It must be a German soldier who was hiding and I am done for." He waited, but no one came. Finally, not hearing any more noise, he decided to investigate. What he saw on the roof was a lost goat munching some grass along the edge of the roof and looking at him, as though she was asking, what is the matter with you; why are you shaking like a leaf?

AC: What a relief!

MR: You bet! But Robert did not come back empty handed that day. He brought us a wheel of cheese that the farmers who owned the chalet, had left. Alain, I remember this delicious cheese. What a feast!

Ethnic Restaurants

The most salient part of ethnicity in the United States is the food that people eat and how they prepare it, in other words, their cuisine. We enjoyed going to Italian, Chinese, Japanese, French, and Mexican restaurants, but I discovered that oftentimes the owners and the people who work at the restaurants do not speak the language that you would expect. For example, I was in the Upper Peninsula of Michigan with some of my cousins. It was dinner time and we stopped to eat at an Italian restaurant where nobody spoke Italian. On the other hand, when we had a condo in Ramona, California, we would eat at an Italian restaurant that was owned by an Italian family. You could even hear famous opera songs in the background while you ate.

In Escondido, not far from Ramona, there was a very good French restaurant. The owners were not French, but the cook (or was he the chef?) was. He had been in the States nine years and was very happy to speak French with me. After we spoke, we shook hands the way the French do and he went back to the kitchen. There are authentic French restaurants in California just as there are in New York or Chicago. A friend invited me to eat at a French restaurant in Berkeley, California, where the owner and the waiter were both French.

A Book from France

For a few years we had a condo in Ramona, California. Once a month, the library raised funds by asking people to donate books that others could buy. Once, I found the book *Babar, the king of the elephants*, which is a famous children's book in France. This copy was even written in French, so I bought it for 50 cents. I wanted to read it to my grandchildren who were very young at the time, They did not know French, but they listened very seriously and if I skipped a page, they made sure to let me know.

When one of my grandsons was five, he brought me a book in English he wanted me to read. But before I started to read, he stopped me and said, "*Grandpere*, you do not know how to read in English. Forget it."

A Fish Stew Story

In the summer of 1984, my cousin Daniel Jouve and his wife Annie decided to come to the United States and take a trip with us to the Gaspe Peninsula, which is in the extreme eastern part of the Quebec province in Canada. When we arrived, I could not believe how French that part of Canada was. People there speak 300-year-old French and few speak English. In the motel we slept at one night, only the owner spoke English. I will never forget that trip because we felt like we were in France instead of Canada. One night after seeing the Northern Lights so brightly—there was no other light pollution to interfere—we decided to find a place for dinner. The owner of the motel told us that we could not eat in his restaurant that particular night because it was reserved for a wedding, but we could eat very well in another restaurant that was within walking distance.

The village we were staying in was a fishing village, so we ordered fish meals. I saw that I could have *bouillabaisse*—a French fish stew. Since I had not eaten *bouillabaisse* in 30 years, I decided to order it. It turned out to be a mistake because my family had to wait a long time to be served. Tired of waiting, I went to the kitchen to ask how much longer it would be, and I was told that it takes a long time to cook a *bouillabaisse*. When I suggested ordering something else the owner of the restaurant told me: "Monsieur ordered *bouillabaisse* and Monsieur will have his *bouillabaisse*." Whether they are in France or in Canada, French people take eating seriously. Nice custom!

Cottage on a Lake

On a summer day in 1985, my wife received a phone call from her daughter Cathy who told her that her father, my wife's ex-husband, was selling his cottage on Wiggins Lake in Michigan. She thought maybe her mother would be interested in buying it. After their divorce, my wife's ex-husband owned the cottage and my wife owned their house in East Lansing, Michigan. On a Saturday morning we went to see the cottage. As soon as my wife saw it, she said, "I'm not in love with the cottage; I'm in love with the lake."

Joanne decided she wanted to see her cousin Sue who lived on the lake since we were already there. So we walked the 300 yards to Sue's house for a visit. Since seeing each other last, both women had become grandmothers and they were sharing in each other's happiness and catching up. As I looked around, I saw that there was a cottage for sale by owner next door. The owner happened to be outside watering his lawn, so I went to talk to him and soon I was inspecting the cottage. I learned that he had built the cottage himself and had not spared any expense while doing so. I was impressed. Sue and Joanne soon came over to ask me what I was doing. I told them I was buying the cottage—I knew that Joanne wanted to have a house on a lake and Wiggins Lake was beautiful with fantastic sunsets, swans, ducks, and frogs. After a discussion with the owner, I bought the cottage. Joanne, me, the kids, and grandkids all had a marvelous time swimming and boating ever since.

5

Teaching

Guess Who Does Not Understand Me When I Speak English?

During my time teaching at MSU, students who did not major in science were required to take a natural science course. Many sections were offered, and I taught three of them. For the first three days of classes, students could change sections for any reason. Some of the professors—including me—were not born in the States and had slight foreign accents. This is where my story comes in. At the beginning of one semester I was talking to my Egyptian colleague when he told me that a young lady changed her section from mine to his because she could not understand me. He even added, "she is French." Ouch.

A Geological Trip to Canada

While teaching natural science to non-science majors, one of the subjects we focused on was geology. One year, the head of our department decided that our students should see the oldest rock formation on earth, which happened to be about 400 miles north of Toronto in Ontario, Canada. We took a university bus to see it. The first person to get on the bus was a colleague of mine named Charles. He had dark skin and told us, "I know I have to ride at the back of the bus." A few minutes later, we were on our way to Toronto where we passed the first night.

Around midnight, my roommate and I were awakened by two young women who told us that we were in their room.

After calling the front desk it was confirmed that our room was first rented to the young women, so we got another room. We made the trip to our new room in our pajamas.

We passed the second night in the small town of Bishop at a hotel that only had one bathroom. We decided that maybe we could skip taking a bath for one day. That evening some people decided to see Bishop's downtown. Charles went and later told me, "We did not see anything out of the ordinary, but the people we met looked at me a lot. Possibly because they have never seen a 'black man' before."

The next day we went to see the oldest rocks in America. It was very interesting, as was our Canadian guide. At one moment, the head of the department, Hackel, and I stood on one side of a cliff, and the other members of the faculty stood on the other. Hackel joking told me, "Al, go on the other side of the cliff and push over the rocks above them. I don't need them on my staff anymore."

During our visit, we collected some rock samples. Upon crossing the border to the United States we were asked if we had anything to declare. We told them only rocks. Then, I do not know why, one guard asked one of the women to open her suitcase. He only found dirty clothes, and then we were back on our way. Once back on campus, we arranged the rocks in a small garden to commemorate our geological trip.

A Human Story

Among the many stories I have from teaching at Michigan State University, this one is special to me. The day before the final, one "black" student of mine, whose surname was "White," told me that he would not be at the final because he had to go to Detroit to prevent his dad from beating his mom. Although he was only eighteen-years-old, he could do that because he was six-foot-two. He said that he would be back on campus the next Monday, and asked if he could take the exam then. I trusted him, so I told him that it was fine. He never forgot me—a few years later I was driving across East Lansing when a police car pulled me over. I stopped, wondering what I could have done wrong, when the police officer approached. He said, "Hi, Dr. Corcos. I just wanted to say hello and see how you are doing." It was my former student in a police uniform!

Birth of a New Course

One of the greatest joys for a professor is to be offered the opportunity to teach a new course that has never been taught by anyone on the campus or possibly ever taught at all. I was struck with this opportunity when my department decided to offer new courses. I proposed to teach one that I called, "The Concept of Race." This course was to be taught from a biological point of view. I taught the course for years, and it remained challenging to me because I was continuously learning about the subject as I taught it.

Students often asked to have copies of old exams because they believed it would help them learn better, but I would not provide any old exams for "The Concept of Race" course. When they asked why, I would answer that it would not do them any good because I changed the answers all the time. They thought it was a bad joke, but it was the truth. As I learned more about the subject, I had to change the answers to many of my questions from one year to the next. One time I even had to stop in the middle of a sentence because I realized that what I was saying didn't make any sense. Only one student asked me why I had stopped.

In 1991, I gave my last lecture, which was on the concept of race. At that time, it was customary for students to comment about the course and instructor on the day of the final. Some students had written this illuminating question: "Dr. Corcos, how come you never defined human race?" Reading this was like lighting striking my brain. If I cannot define human races, there must be a reason: they might not exist. I determined that human races were a biological myth, and I was not alone in that conclusion. The American Anthropology society wrote a statement to that effect in 1992, but I was the first to write a book for college students and the public at large about it. My book, *The Myth of Human Races* was published after my retirement so I never used it in my classes. However, it has been used on some other university campuses. It was also used at MSU one summer by an instructor who taught outstanding high school students from inner-city Detroit the summer before their freshman year of college. On the last day of the program, I was invited to answer questions and sign their copies of the book. I remember that one student posed this question to me: "My father is black and my mother is white. When I am asked on official papers if I am black or white, I don't want to offend my parents because I love them. What should I do?" I answered, "I see a good-looking young woman, who is neither black nor white, and you should answer the question: 'To what race do you belong?' with the word 'human.'"

Problems Teaching Human Genetics

The following story is about the consequences of teaching human genetics—in particular blood types and genetic diseases. Sometimes students discover that they are adopted, they are not actually identical twins, or that they have the diseases you describe in your lectures.

One day in Monmouth, I was teaching the inheritance of blood groups. After the lecture, a young lady came to my office and asked if there were exceptions about the inheritance of blood groups. I told her that I did not know of any. Then she said, "This confirms what I suspected for a long time…." I started to shake in my boots. What personal story she was going to share with me? She continued, "One night when I was ten, my mother and grandmother were talking about me. They thought I was asleep but I was not, and I heard them say that I was adopted. Since then, I learned that both of my parents have blood type O and I have blood type A. From the information in your lecture, I am not their biological child. Is that correct?" I answered, "Yes, and what are you going to about it?" I was still shaking. She quickly answered, "Nothing. They are excellent parents, and I am going to get married this Tuesday." Boy was I relieved.

There are many blood groups; among them is the Rh group that sometimes presents a problem. If a woman is Rh- and the father of her child is Rh+, their child could be aborted if that child's blood type happens to be Rh+. While I was a professor at Michigan State University, I had a nursing student in class whose blood type was Rh-. She told me after my lecture that she had solved her own problem. Before going on a date, she would ask her companion his blood type. If he was Rh+, he would be out of luck. Her decision decreased her chances of finding her Prince Charming by 85% because only 15% of males in the United States are blood type Rh-.

For many years we had a lab section that accompanied the lecture on blood groups in which the students learned how to check their own blood types. The worst part was that many students did not want to prick their fingers.

In one class I had a nursing student who wanted to practice pricking fingers. She told her schoolmates to line up and she would do it for them—she had a lot of customers!

In one class, I had a young man who was about six-foot-two who would faint at the sight of blood. I was ready for this scenario—I had ammonia in a container, which I brought to his nose. At its smell, the student woke up and leapt to his feet. Later, a student told me, "Dr. Corcos, you did very well in that situation. I know because I am a medic." My first thought was, "Why on earth didn't he help me?" That was my first time 'reviving' a student.

This type of lab was canceled after the discovery of AIDS, because we were concerned about transmitting the disease.

The French Section

I taught required natural science courses to non-science majors for several years. One particular year, the son of the department chair told his father that all his courses were in French the next term, except his natural science course. His father told him that a French section could be arranged because there was an instructor in the department who happened to be French—that was me!

Once classes started, I was excited to see that not only had his son enrolled in my section, but an additional ten other students as well. Some of them spoke multiple languages. Among the students was a French girl named Nicole whose parents had a French restaurant in New York. It was impossible to tell whether she was French or American. There was also a girl who became a famous singer, named Sally Rodger. I had the pleasure of seeing her sing her years later. There was also a boy from Vietnam who told me that I had a strange accent. I had a lot of fun teaching that section. When I asked a question in French, I was sometimes answered in Russian or some other language. Two weeks before the final, I told them that the final would be in English and they better know what

I had taught them. On exam day, I was told that they all got together to study as they ate hot dogs and drank beer. All of them passed the course.

President Clinton

I saw former president Bill Clinton in the summer of 1995 when he gave the commencement address at Michigan State University. His security detail was everywhere—even on the tops of buildings. But there was something curious on the platform: one more dean than usual. It turned out that he was just posing as a dean and was actually Clinton's bodyguard. I saw him again on TV when Clinton was in Moscow two weeks later. To me, President Clinton is more handsome when you see him in person than when you see him on TV. The same could be said about President John F. Kennedy.

More Stories About Teaching

The following story happened about 40 years ago, but could have happened today. Young students just out of high school cannot wait to get to college because, for most of them, it is the first time that they are really free from their parents' influences.

Just a few minutes before 8 a.m. on the first day of classes, I arrived in my classroom to find a young lady already sitting in the first row. She looked at me strangely. After a minute, I asked her what was wrong. She replied: "I leave home to go to college and on the first day, in my first class on campus, my first instructor looks exactly like my Dad." I told her I was sorry.

Another time, as I was lecturing, a student fell asleep—there might have been more than one over the years—but this one started to snore heavily. I asked his neighbor to awaken him. When he did, I asked the class to answer a question about something I just said. The only student to answer my question was the sleepy one. My ego was really hurt that day.

Once I had a student who was flunking my course and I was astonished because he did not seem like the type to fail. I told him so, and I will never forget his answer: "Dr. Corcos, you assume that I want to pass your course, but I don't. I want to show my Dad that I am not college material. All I want is to become a professional golfer." He left me astonished and wondering how many students were just like him.

Another time when I was an advisor, I was astonished to learn that one of my advisees had five As at the end of his first term. While checking into his background, I learned that he had been a C-student in high school. A few days later I was discussing this with him and he told me, "In high school I didn't try, but now I am in college and that is another story." I soon lost my advisee to the Honor College.

At the end of one term I had a young lady tell me, "I'm mad because my high school didn't prepare me for college. This Friday is welcome back home day [at the high school] and I am going to tell the principal what I think." Good luck, lady!

———————

One term I had a male student who continuously asked stupid questions. I know there are no stupid questions, but let's just say that the answers to these questions were painfully obvious. Later in the term, I was completely astonished to find that this student had the best score on the final exam (a multiple-choice test). The day after the final I saw him on campus and told him the good news. He answered: "You seem astonished. You must think I'm stupid." No comment.

———————

Sometimes college students are not ready to find out that their ideas of the world are not those of scientists or historians. A "white" student asked me why her sister had characteristics that you generally attribute to a "black" person. I replied that she could possibly have black ancestors. She blew up at me and said angrily, "How dare you say that my family has black ancestors." She was absolutely furious and even went to see the head of my department to complain about me. She was told that there was something called freedom of ideas on campus and if she didn't want to be exposed to new ideas and concepts, she should consider leaving Michigan State University.

6

My Career

I Could Have Been Famous

At the end of my life, I can say that I am truly happy that I was a scientist. Professionally, I was lucky to do research on molecular biology just shortly after its discovery, which was a very exciting period for the field. The only regret I have is that if I had possessed more of an imagination, I would have been the first to discover that a virus' chromosomes were circular rather than longitudinal. My experimental data was telling me just that—unfortunately I did not make the correct interpretation. Here is my story.

While working at the University of California at Santa Barbara, my colleague and friend Eduardo Orias and I were attempting to get temperature-sensitive mutants of a virus called P22 that attacks and destroys Salmonella typhmurium. Virus temperature-sensitive mutants are viruses that can replicate, let's say, at 25º C, but not at 37º C. We obtained two mutants.

Geneticists like to know how far apart mutations fall on the chromosome, so I used the usual method to determine this. However, I found something strange. One day I found that the distance was 2 map units and on another day, it was 22 map units. I repeated the experiment many times. The results were always the same, but they did not make any sense to me, and I blamed myself. I should have given myself more leniency because I later learned why it did not make sense: I was assuming the chromosome of a virus was longitudinal like those in humans or fruit flies. But if I were to suppose that the chromosome of a virus is circular, the distance between two mutations would depend on where the chromosome breaks—chromosomes break all the time when they replicate. If the P22 virus chromosome breaks between the sites of the two mutations, the distance would be 22 map units and if the break occurs outside the mutations, the distance would be 2 map units, which are exactly the results I was getting. Unfortunately, I did not have the imagination to hypothesize that viruses could have circular chromosomes. This fact was discovered a few years later.

Two decades later, I talked about my "near fame" in finding this very important biological discovery in one of my lectures to non-science majors. My students told me that it was the best lecture I had ever given. They finally understood what science is all about.

About Turkeys

I write this story a week before Thanksgiving 2022. Every thanksgiving I am reminded of a trip I took to Boulder, Colorado in 1967, to attend a scientific meeting of biologists. I was having breakfast when a man asked me if it was alright for him to sit at my table. We got to talking, and soon I learned that he was a turkey breeder for the USDA. The problem with turkey breeding, he told me, was that there is a limit to the size of the chest of a turkey. If the chest is too big, the bird falls over. Even the turkey breeders have reached a limit. What are they going to do next?

An Original Idea in the History of Science

In 1983, a colleague and friend of mine named Floyd Monaghan retired. Soon after retirement, he discovered that he did not know what to do with all his time, even though he had a few hobbies. One day he came to see me and told me that he wanted to help me with my research. I accepted even though he was a chemist rather than a plant biologist. A few months later, he came and told me that he had read Gregor Mendel's famous paper, which led to the new science of genetics. He pointed out that this paper is always quoted, but never read. He was surprised that he couldn't find the word "heredity" anywhere in the paper and asked me to read it to be sure. I could not find the word either, which lend us to wonder why Mendel is called the Father of Genetics.

After reading his article, I found that he was an even better scientist than I had thought, as well as an excellent mathematician. I am sure that the reason his paper was ignored was because few of his contemporaries, if any, could understand his mathematical explanation of his ratio results. Floyd had an original idea about this, which led us to write 20 articles about Gregor Mendel and the discoveries noted in his article from 1900. Our articles were published in the *Journal of Heredity*, and we also wrote a book explaining his work called *Gregor Mendel's Experiments on Plant Hybrids: A Guided Study*.[7] We explained that Mendel was looking for the laws of hybridization, not the laws of heredity. The irony is

---

7   Alain F. Corcos and Floyd Monaghan. *Gregor Mendel's Experiments on Plant Hybrids' A Guided Study.* (Rutgers University Press, N.J), 1993.

that if he had searched for the laws of heredity, he would have done the same experiments. Because of this, I think he can keep his title of "Father of Genetics." Our book is still quoted often, even 30 years after it was published. Ironically, Floyd never knew his fame. He died in 1992 at the age of 85.

Arabidopsis Thaliana

Gregor Mendel, the Father of Genetics, worked with peas for his experiments, but the early geneticists worked with the fruit fly. One of the reasons for this is that it takes only ten days for the fruit fly to reproduce. Geneticists are known to be impatient with the results of their experiments and therefore prefer to work with fungi, bacteria, and viruses, which reproduce within minutes.

Though the fruit fly was found quickly, it took years to find the model organism in plant biology. Once found, this plant was marvelous to work with because it only has 5 pairs of large chromosomes, a rapid life cycle, and prolific seed production. It can grow in test tubes or Petri dishes and can be genetically transformed utilizing Agrobacterium tumefaciens.

My story has to do with the history of Arabidopsis thaliana. It was discovered in the sixteenth century by Johannes Thal in the Harz Mountains. Hundreds of years later in 1943, Friedrich Laibach first summarized the potential of Arabidopsis thaliana as a model organism in genetics. One of the pioneers in this research was George Rédei, whom I met in the late 1960s at his home in Columbia, Missouri. He was a Hungarian scientist who immigrated to the United States in 1958 with his wife when the Soviet Union invaded Hungary. This was his adventure:

He and his wife escaped from Hungary and reached the U.S. Embassy in Vienna, Austria, where they learned that the U.S. government would accept 1,000 Hungarian refugees. It just so happened that George was the 1,000th— but what about his wife? Well, the U.S. authorities decided to accept Mrs. Rédei as the 1,001st. So the next day, they both flew to Baltimore, Maryland. Upon arrival they were asked what specific job they wanted to pursue. George shyly told them he wanted any job that involved plants. So the authorities started to call every agricultural experimental station in every state. When they reached one in Columbia, Missouri, they got the Dean of the College of Agriculture, who discussed the idea of hiring Rédei with another professor in the college. When the name "Rédei" came up, the professor told the dean, "You better get him right away. He sent me an excellent article." So the dean sent $100 to George so he could buy an airplane ticket to Columbia. But, again, what about his wife? Well the people around Mrs. Rédei put some money in a hat and soon she had enough to also buy a plane ticket. Once in Columbia, they stayed in the basement of the Dean's house for a month, at which time the Dean was finally able to secure the money to hire George as a professor in the crop department. He remained there until he retired. George had come to the States with only a shirt and a pair of pants, but guess what he had in his right pocket? Seeds of Arabidopsis, which would end up being used in all the Arabidopsis labs in the U.S., and possibly all over the world.

During our visit, Professor Rédei gave me some Arabidopsis thaliana seeds and I went home to start my research with this jewel of a plant. I saw George Rédei once more in 1976, when we were both invited to give papers and chaired meetings at the Second International Congress of Arabidopsis in Frankfort, Germany.

7

Our Vacations

Our First Cruise

The destination of our first cruise was Alaska. We met a lot of people on the ship and among them was a nice couple who were also on their first cruise. The wife had just buried her mother whom she had taken care of for months. She was exhausted and decided she wanted to do absolutely nothing for a few days—so why not take a cruise? On a cruise you are taken care of, eat well, always entertained, and you get to see beautiful things. She bought two tickets and then told her husband about the trip He was very surprised and immediately bought a video camera to record everything they saw. At the time, video cameras were very large. One afternoon, close to 6 p.m., we were anchored in Juneau and the husband discovered that he had to recharge his video camera. He entered a random building and found a bathroom with a plug to charge the camera. As he was waiting for the charge, a janitor came in and told him that he was in the governor's bathroom. He said it was alright as long as he closed the door after he was finished.

Our Plane Is Here, But...

Years ago, my wife and I decided to visit Hawaii to see this beautiful part of the U.S. We thought that the best way to see it was to take a cruise along the islands. After all, we were on vacation and we wanted to relax.

Our first step was to take a plane from Lansing, Michigan, to Chicago, Illinois. We arrived without problems in the

Windy City, and our plane to Honolulu waiting for us. Everything looked fine, but we soon found out that it was not. We learned that something was wrong with the plane engine and we had to wait for another plane. All 300 of us waited two hours, at which point we were told to go and eat a free lunch. As time ticked by, we started to worry that we would miss our ship that was set to leave Honolulu at 7:30 p.m.

After hours of waiting, we were finally told that two planes, not one, would take us to San Francisco and then one more plane, a DC 10 would take us to Hawaii. We were also told that our luggage was already on its way through Los Angeles, which was very assuring. When we finally arrived in Honolulu, we saw a few people with placards for the cruise passengers. We were told to rapidly follow them to take a special bus to the harbor where our ship was waiting for the eleven of us.

As we arrived onboard, we were welcomed by the other passengers who had given us the nickname, "the gang of Chicago." As soon as we were onboard, the ship took off. And guess what! Our luggage was in front of our cabin door. After that hiccup, we thoroughly enjoyed the rest of our vacation.

Eruption of the Kilauea Volcano

During another cruise we took around the Hawaiian Islands in 1984, we saw an eruption of the very active Kilauea volcano. We first saw it at night and thought it was just an illuminated town in the distance, but it turned out that all the lights we could see were actually lava burning everything in its path. It was a beautiful spectacle, but very destructive.

We saw the most active and youngest volcano in Hawaii many times. Scientists estimate that Kilauea, a 4,090-foot-tall mountain, began forming on the ocean floor between 300,000 and 600,000 years ago and appeared above sea level between 50,000 and 100,000 years ago. The most recent and longest eruption began in 1983 and continued into the 21st century.

Another time we were not able to go ashore in Hawaii was when the National Park was closed due to a government shutdown. Instead of going to see the park, the captain of the cruise ship decided to show us Pearl Harbor and the monument instead. We were reminded of the Pearl Harbor bombing by the Japanese Air Force on the December 7, 1941, and were asked if any of us were on the island that day. Three former navymen had been there. Then we were asked to stand if we were veterans of World War II—there were many. I did not get up until my wife reminded me: "Did you forget that you are a veteran of World War II?" The problem was that I was in the French Air Force, not the American Air Force, and despite being a U.S. citizen, I did not think of myself as a U.S. veteran. I got up just in time.

The Panama Canal

My wife and I went on many cruises with the Holland America Cruise line. We even found out something interesting about their policy: If you came just about thirty minutes before the ship departs and it's not full, you might be able to get a cheap room. However, we never took advantage of this, even though it would have been possible—we have a daughter in San Diego so lodging was cheap.

I believe the most interesting cruise we took was down the Panama Canal. I had a very vague idea of what it could be like before we went. I did not know that there were three lakes along the canal and that it took practically a day to go through them because of how slowly the ship moved. I was also astonished at how narrow the last lock was; our cruise ship barely made it through! Today the canal has been enlarged and I am sure that it costs more to cross than when we went—$50,000.

The Submarine

In my book, *The Little Yellow Train*, I mentioned that I nearly went in a submarine to join the Free French under General de Gaulle. That all changed at the last minute because the man in charge of getting me on the submarine was shot. German Intelligence discovered that he was a British citizen, even though he was an officer in the German Army.

Years later I got to go in a submarine while on a Hawaiian cruise with my wife—an adventure that no one should miss. The sight of the abundant ocean life is something that has no equal on land. We enjoyed it thoroughly. I remember that the tickets cost us $200. We went 100 feet under the ocean—$1 a foot!

The Last Story

My wife and I took our last cruise in 2015 accompanied by two of our daughters, Karen and Cathy. We went to Alaska, and one night we joined a few strangers at a table for dinner. As usual we introduced ourselves. When it came to me, I said I was born and raised in France. Immediately upon sharing this information, a man—let us call him Joe—at the table started speaking to me in French. He told me that he passed 10 years of his life in France including four years during World War II, when he had been part of the underground. I told him I had contacts with the Resistance, and we decided to exchange room numbers so we could pursue our conversation the next morning.

The morning came, but no Joe. I called his room and he told me that he was coming, but he never did. I started to wonder why he did not want to talk. It took me three days to find a possible excuse: I had told him I had contacts with the underground, and Joe might not have actually been in the underground. Perhaps he was afraid that I would find out. Could it be that he invented his story? In any case, I never talked with Joe after that dinner, but I saw him when we left the ship. He saw me too, for he raised his arm to wave goodbye. I did not return the wave.

Conclusion

Our Life Could Have Been Different

In a book—I cannot remember which one—I read that in 1923, the Spanish government made a historic decision to grant Spanish citizenship to the descendants of Jews who were expelled from Spain in 1492. This was not well known. Yet, it seems that some thousands of European Jews were saved from the holocaust by claiming Spanish citizenship. They had Sephardic names. And so is the Corcos name. But we did not know anything about this in 1940 when Father was sure that Jews and those who have Jewish ancestry were destined to be Hitler's victims. It is interesting to note that we could have become Spanish citizens without speaking Spanish and we did not need to stay in Spain. If we had known we would have gone to the Spanish embassy and registered. And guess what! I would not have written *The Little Yellow Train Survival and Escape from Nazi France.*